WONDERS OF MAN

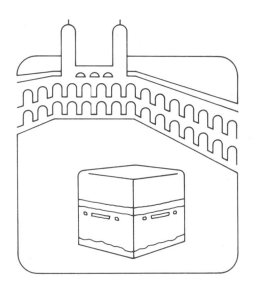

MECCA

by **Desmond Stewart**

Photographs by Mohamed Amin

NEWSWEEK, New York

Fairview Lets. 09

NEWSWEEK BOOK DIVISION

Edwin D. Bayrd, Jr.   *Editor*
Mary Ann Joulwan   *Art Director*
Valerie Brooks   *Managing Editor*
Laurie P. Winfrey   *Picture Editor*
Eva Galan   *Copy Editor*

Alvin Garfin   *Publisher*

WONDERS OF MAN

Milton Gendel   *Consulting Editor*

ENDSHEETS: *Following in the footsteps of the Veiled Prophet, Muhammad, whose legendary Pilgrimage of Farewell occurred in A.D. 632, pious Muslims pour into Mecca during the season of the hajj. Their number, which has risen steadily over the centuries, now exceeds two million annually— turning the narrow streets into a seething sea of the faithful.*

TITLE PAGE: *Encircled by the two-tier arcade of the Sacred Mosque and overshadowed by its twin minarets, the black-draped Kaaba seems singularly unimposing. Size is no measure of sanctity, however, and the world's 800 million Muslims regard this simple stone cube as the holiest of holies and the nexus of their zealously held faith.*

OPPOSITE: *Iridescent blues may predominate on this eighteenth-century Turkish tile, but the eye is drawn inexorably to the inky shape at the center, instantly identifiable as the Kaaba.*

Photographs © 1980 Mohamed Amin

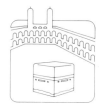

Printed and bound in Japan.

Contents

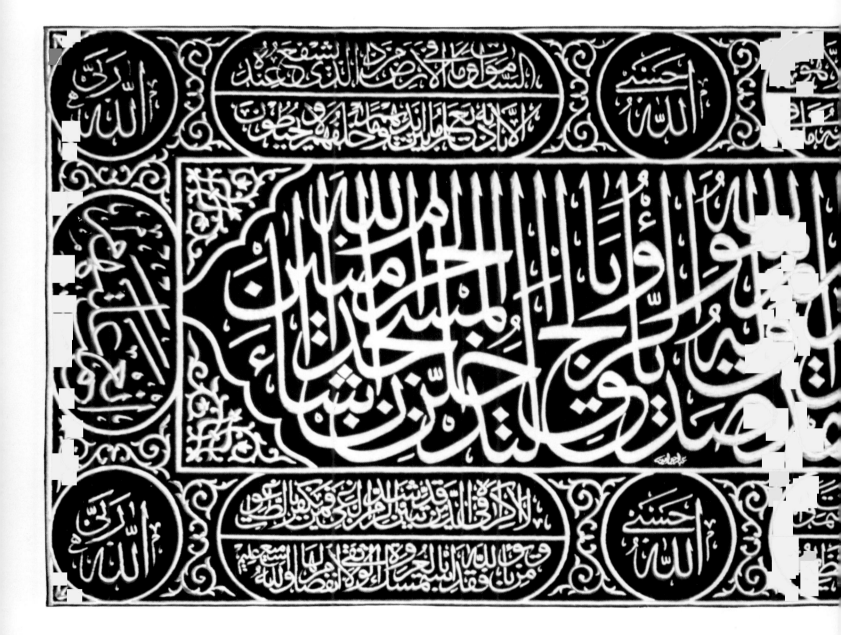

Introduction

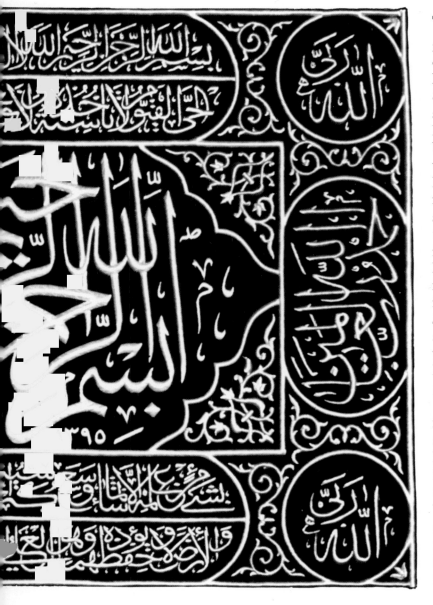

The city of Mecca is a striking anomaly among great religious centers, for it offers little in the way of magnificent art or monumental architecture to lure the faithful yet it exerts a pull on the world's 800 million Muslims that beggars the emotional sway of any other sacred site. Lhasa and Lourdes, Benares and Borobudur, Chartres and Canterbury—each has its special appeal, but none can rival Mecca, which serves as a spiritual magnet for Muslims from Trinidad to Tashkent. Millions make the annual pilgrimage to Mecca during the sacred month of Dhul-Hijja, temporarily trading their distinctive national costumes for the anonymity of the *hajji*'s white robes. And hundreds of millions more prostrate themselves toward Mecca five times a day, acknowledging the holy city and its devotional epicenter, the Kaaba, as Islam's *kiblah*, or focus of prayer. (The vast drapery that enshrouds the Kaaba is familiar to every Muslim, whether he or she has made the *hajj* or not. A richly embroidered segment from that drapery's calligraphic frieze is seen at left.)

Mecca is unexampled in another respect as well, for unlike Ise, Jerusalem, or the Vatican, it is proscribed to non-believers—and has been since Muhammad took the city for Islam in A.D. 630. Foreign visitors have entered Mecca from time to time, but only in disguise and only at their peril. Through this volume, access to Mecca becomes universal and unrestricted: readers are given an unparalleled opportunity to inspect the holy city from the vantage of the pilgrim and from the longer perspective of history.

THE EDITORS

11

MECCA IN HISTORY

I

The Navel of the World

Among the planet's khaki deserts Arabia is remarkable for its shape, size, and influence on human history. A wedge more than a million square miles in extent—and thus the world's largest peninsula—it splits Africa from Asia, being washed on the east by the Persian Gulf, on the south by the Indian Ocean, and on the west by the bright blue trough of the misnamed Red Sea (see map, page 19). Arabia has given its language to two dozen members of the United Nations and contributed loan words to other languages, including English. The peninsula's inhabitants have named it the Island of the Arabs. The name is appropriate, if inaccurate, since its vastness and desolation have kept it more insular than many islands; invaders from the Romans to the Turks have found its sands more obstructive than the oceans.

The peninsula's western rampart—whose name, Hijaz, means barrier—rises from a narrow coastal plain. To passing ships the mountainous escarpment of the Hijaz presents a savage beauty; to those traveling on land, stony dearth. This barrier stretches from Sinai in the north to the uplands of Yemen, kept green by monsoon rains, in the southwest—and thereby shuts off the steppe of central Arabia from the sea. It is the north, where the "island" slopes into western Asia, that provides a causeway, both for the introduction of foreign ideas and the emigration of surplus people. Throughout history the desert nomads of the peninsula made sorties into Syria and Babylonia, prompted sometimes by greed, more often by drought. These sorties were to reach their historical climax in the seventh century, when, in a giant eruption largely powered by dedication to a new religion, the Arabians surged from their deserts to propagate a faith that now influences some seven hundred million people—a faith that has inspired a dozen cultures.

This vast and empty land has never possessed a hublike metropolis from which populous thoroughfares could radiate to other cities. Yet one city, set in the tangled hills of the western escarpment, has played a unique role in Arabia and, because of Arabia's influence on history, in the world at large. Known to Ptolemy, the classical geographer, as Macoraba, from a word meaning sanctuary, and to the Arabs as Mecca, this city owed its early importance to several identifiable factors. Set in an amphitheatre of barren hills about fifty miles inland from the sea, it possessed a well of abundant water. Moreover, this water was drinkable, although many have found it unpalatable (and some, unhealthy). The well, known as Zemzem, facilitated the establishment of a permanent settlement, which contrasted both with the temporary encampments of the nomads, who moved on when the greenery resulting from capricious rainstorms withered, and with the smaller groups of dwellings supported by the other oases that pocked the wilderness.

Unlike most such oases, Mecca occupied a geographical position in the ocean of sand that was to prove as crucial as Venice's position at the head of the Adriatic Sea or New York's at the mouth of the Hudson River. At Mecca, two major caravan routes converged. One, running west to east, linked Africa by way of the Arabian steppe to Iran and Central Asia. The other, running southeast to northwest, enabled the incense and spices of southern Arabia and India to be ferried into the Mediterranean basin, supplementing the risky sea route to the east that had been discovered by the Romans. This advantageous position enabled the Meccans

not merely to exist but to accumulate wealth.

A third asset, originally rivaling the other two but eventually surpassing them—and, in the process, winning this dusty city, nestled in beige, treeless hills, its permanent importance—was an unusual building. At the narrow valley's lowest point, close to the well that watered the city, a temple had stood from time immemorial. Its appearance and function have changed throughout the centuries, but not its basic shape. An almost square structure of granite blocks, the Kaaba owes its name to the Arabic word for cube or dice. Pious legend was later to claim that the Kaaba had existed in Heaven before the Creation and that Adam had reconstructed it on earth according to God's directions. A Black Stone enshrined at the site was said to have been presented by the Angel Gabriel. This circular stone, probably a meteorite, may have suggested the description of the Kaaba as the navel of the world (a psychologically understandable connection: the pagan Greeks made the same claim for the Omphalos, a sacred stone preserved at Delphi). Later legend was also to insist that the Kaaba had originally been a place of monotheistic worship that had later declined into polytheistic superstition. As a pagan temple the Kaaba was hung with the pelts of sacrificed animals, and the custom of covering its grayish stone has been continued to this day. Different colored cloth has been used—it was green when a traveler visited Mecca from Moorish Spain in 1184—but the black employed in recent centuries seems impressively appropriate. The somber color strikes a note of emphasis in a landscape of saffron and brown. Two-thirds of the way up, a frieze embroidered in golden calligraphy relieves the blackness.

Alterations far more radical than mere changes in the color of its hangings have affected the shrine over the centuries. In the last years of Arabian paganism, Mecca's financial oligarchs built mansions close to what was then a temple without a precinct. Lanes between these houses gave worshipers access to the shrine. Sacred stones and idols crammed the interior of the Kaaba and in all likelihood pressed against its external walls. The mansions have long since been pulled down and an open space capable of holding half a million worshipers now surrounds the Kaaba. And except for the Black Stone, no obvious trace of paganism survives. Yet despite this simplification, the Kaaba's renown has constantly increased. Throughout every hour of the day and night men and women circumambulate the cyclopean structure, moving in a counterclockwise direction from the Black Stone, which those who can get near enough kiss—and those who cannot, salute. In the colonnades that surround the open precinct the pious have traditionally slumbered, one eye open for the privilege of becoming the solitary worshiper making this ritual circuit. But so constant is the stream of worshipers to the focal point of the world's second largest monotheistic faith that the privilege is rarely won. Even if no man were present, it is believed, the Kaaba would be thronged: seventy thousand angels are said to circle the shrine in company with mortals. When wind rustles the black covering, its movement is thought to be evidence of this celestial attendance. Nor is the Kaaba honored only in Mecca and within the sacred precinct. Ever since Mecca's noblest son, the Prophet Muhammad, delivered God's command—"Turn then thy face in the direction of the Sacred Mosque: wherever ye are,

Five times each day the muezzins call, and each time roughly one quarter of the earth's population prostrates itself toward Mecca. These daily prayers—rightly described as the greatest single act of devotion on earth—unite Muslims everywhere in a communality of action and intent that transcends cultural differences and geographical distances. The marble-walled precincts of the Sacred Mosque can hold half a million worshipers, but during the height of the pilgrimage season, the overflow fills every open space in the city.

turn your faces in that direction!''—untold millions from all continents have prostrated themselves five times a day toward this magnetic center known as Bayt-allah, God's House. The first occasion, proclaimed by graybeards from minarets, occurs before dawn lights the east, and the last is after sunset.

The religion of which this shrine is the *kiblah*, or focus for prayer, has as its symbol the *hilal*, or crescent moon; its calendar is still based on the lunar year of ancient Arabia. The Meccans of pagan times periodically inserted extra days into their calendar, and this kept the lunar months in rough accord with the solar seasons. This is no longer the case. The lunar year loses some eleven days annually in solar terms, coming back to the same solar time in a cycle of thirty-three years. At a fixed point in this wandering lunar year, coming sometimes in burning August, at others in cooler December, pilgrims converge in multitudes on Mecca from all points of the compass. In the first half of the lunar month of Dhul-Hijja they come to take part in the *hajj*, or major pilgrimage, which culminates in the Feast of Sacrifice, the major holiday in the Islamic year.

Like many European cathedrals, the Kaaba commands a site once linked to a pagan cult. This sacred territory, or *haram*, has expanded since ancient times to include not just the area around the Kaaba but the entire city of Mecca and the surrounding complex of dry valleys, known in Arabic as *wadis*. Whatever its perimeters, the *haram* was governed by traditional taboos against the taking of life, human and animal, or even the picking of its scant indigenous vegetation. Like the inner courtyards of the great temple in first-century Jerusalem, this sacred territory eventually came to be held as forbidden to those who were not members of the religion which held it sacred. In the Jerusalem temple an inscription warned intruders that they faced the death penalty if they passed a certain point; the main highway to Mecca carries placards even today announcing that it is prohibited for non-Muslims. Modern Mecca is amply provided with air-conditioned hotels as well as cheaper accommodations, but the city excludes the foreign tourist who, with his camera and credit card, has become one symbol of our restless century. Although deriving its income from visitors, and having a "season" as much as any ski resort or spa, Mecca remains a city whose significance is religious, not aesthetic or cultural. For his part, the tourist misses little by his exclusion. Except for the Kaaba, whose massive centrality in an open space makes it unforgettable, Mecca contains no major art, even though the religion which it commands has excelled in an architecture blending delicacy with strength. The great builders of Islam worked elsewhere: planting the pillar forests that characterize the seventh-century mosque of Kairouan in Tunisia and the Great Mosque (now the cathedral) of Cordoba in southern Spain; rearing the domes that dominate the skyline of Istanbul and the intricate minarets that punctuate the flat huddle of Cairo's roofs; and evoking fantasies in stone and water, such as Agra's Taj Mahal, or in coral, such as the mosques of Kenya's Indian Ocean coastline.

For all its grandeur, the Kaaba cannot compete in significance with the pattern of Stonehenge or the mass of the Pyramids. Nor would tourists savor a climate that has perennially driven the city's richer residents to seek relief in the nearby mountain resort of Ta'if, where, six

*Inhabitants of the globe's largest peninsula refer to
their million square miles of sandy wastes and arid
uplands as the Island of the Arabs—and in every sense
but the topographical, Arabia is just that. Its
forbidding landscape and punishing heat have proved
a surer barricade to conquest than walls or water, and
until the discovery, in this century, of vast lakes of
black gold beneath its golden sands, Arabia offered
little to tempt invaders. As a result Mecca, which lies a
mere forty miles from the Red Sea coast, has enjoyed
extended periods of political stability—an island of
tranquillity within the larger Island of the Arabs.*

thousand feet above the sea, springs and cooler air foster rich vegetation. A Devon boy, Joseph Pitts, was captured by Algerian pirates in the late seventeenth century and outwardly converted by his master, who took him on a pilgrimage to Mecca. After his later escape to England, Pitts recalled heat so intense that it forced people to run from one side of the street to another. Yet ironically this arid city's chief danger has come, when not from men, from too much water. Storms can be sudden and devastating. One such felled the Kaaba's walls and ruined most of the city in the same century that Pitts made his pilgrimage—which explains why no houses as old as, say, those of Shakespeare's London survive in Mecca. A Swiss, John Lewis Burckhardt, reached Mecca in disguise at the time of Napoleon's downfall and encountered a downpour:

> The water poured down in torrents from the mountains;
> and when the hail ceased, after about an hour, we found
> that the rain, which still continued, had covered the
> Wady Noman with a sheet of water three feet deep,
> while streams of nearly five feet in breadth crossed the
> road with an impetuosity which rendered it impossible
> for us to pass them. In this situation we could neither
> advance nor retreat, knowing that similar currents would
> have been formed in our rear; we therefore took post on
> the side of the mountain, where we were sure of not being washed away, and where we could wait in security
> till the subsiding of the storm. The mountains, however,
> soon presented on their sides innumerable cascades,
> and the inundation became general; while the rain, accompanied with thunder and lightning, continued with
> undiminished violence.

More than a thousand years earlier a pagan poet had concluded a famous ode with a description of a typical Arabian storm. A mountain peak cluttered with the torrent's detritus resembled "the top of a spindle encircled with wool," while the storm littered the level desert "like a merchant of Yemen alighting with his bales of rich apparel." Something extreme, even apocalyptic in the climate seems to infuse the scripture revealed in Mecca: "We roll up the heavens like a scroll," says the Koran, meaning that God foresees the Day of Judgment, a time when "Men will be like moths scattered about and the mountains like carded wool." The sanctity and intensity of this revelation—the motive force behind the religion known as Islam—has established the particular dialect of Mecca as the standard for classical Arabic—much as the King James Bible did for English. Mecca was also to contribute most of its leading men and some of its women to the historical explosion which, thirteen and a half centuries ago, carried an Arabian version of monotheism deep into the Persian and Byzantine empires. Within a single century speakers of the Meccan dialect were encamped north of the Pyrenees in the west and by the frontiers of China in the east, while Caliphs from Mecca ruled an empire larger than Rome's from a new capital in Damascus.

Yet for Arabia and Mecca this victory was bought at a cost. The peninsula lost through emigration its most vigorous stock; the nomadic way of life and the freedom it made possible were transformed; and Mecca's material rewards were scant. It was never to join Damascus and Baghdad in the list of caliphal capitals. It was not to boast a provincial court or major institute of learning. It was to lose its purely Arabic character, re-

The Kaaba, which originally housed pagan idols and tribal totems, has been the chief object of Muslim veneration for 1,500 years, measured by Islam's lunar calendar. Its name, derived from the Arabic word for cube, has been descriptive from the first, although the present cube is somewhat larger than the one that existed in the Prophet's day. That squat, roofless structure burned to the ground in Muhammad's youth and was rebuilt several times thereafter—always on the same site and along the same lines. Thus we have little trouble recognizing the Kaaba—its calligraphic frieze, its high-set door, its gold drainspout—even in this schematic fifteenth-century tourist map.

cruiting its population from the polyglot and polychrome visitors to the Kaaba. It was also to lose its traditional virtues, often replacing hospitality with rapacity and manliness with vice. But as a city linked with every detail of the birth of the new faith, Mecca was to win an enduring role in the religion whose expansion in the nineteenth and twentieth centuries has been as dramatic as its conquests in the seventh. As *kiblah,* or focus of this faith, it exerts a stronger hold over more human emotions than any other single place on earth.

It was this aspect of the forbidden city, and not its unpredictable weather, that most impressed the Swiss traveler Burckhardt. He carried with him the intellectual and scientific equipment of one who had graduated from German and British universities at the dawn of the industrial revolution. The early nineteenth century was a time when European values were unquestioned, at least by Europeans, and Burckhardt was in no sense a convert to the religion whose center he was to describe more tellingly than any Western predecessor. Yet the accent of awe can clearly be heard when he describes the effect of Mecca on the believing Muslim. Late at night, in the shrine that he had risked death to investigate and measure, he sat among the multitude induced by the cool breeze to linger in the open area, which was illuminated by thousands of lamps. Although young—and destined to die only three years later at the age of thirty-three—Burckhardt was no Western naïf, beguiled by the East. He had dismissed the Meccans as "united in the design of cheating the pilgrims" and had characterized their city as "more deficient than any other eastern city of the same size" in things of beauty. Something of a Puritan, he had, like countless Muslims

before him, castigated the immorality that contaminated "the temple of Mekka itself by practices of the grossest depravity: to these no disgrace is here attached; the young of all classes are encouraged in them by the old, and even parents have been so base as to connive at them for the sake of money." Yet neither was Burckhardt so jaundiced as to miss Mecca's impact on the pious. As he watched one night, a pilgrim from Darfour in the remote Sudan suddenly strode into the shrine. It was the last night of Ramadan, the month in which the Koran was first revealed and in which the faithful fast during the daylight hours. "After a long journey across barren and solitary deserts, on his entering the illuminated temple, he was so much struck with its appearance, and overawed by the black Kaaba, that he fell prostrate close by the place where I was sitting, and remained long in that posture of adoration," the Swiss recorded. "He then rose, burst into a flood of tears, and in the height of his emotion, instead of reciting the usual prayers of the visitor, only exclaimed, 'O God, now take my soul, for this is Paradise!'"

Such emotion—along with bottles of Zemzem water for friends and a shroud steeped in the same water for themselves—is what generations of Muslim pilgrims have taken home from Mecca with them.

II

Arabia Before the Prophet

The Age of Ignorance: with this blanket term the Arabs implicitly condemn their history before Muhammad and Islam. To secular historians, however, the label is both a simplification and an exaggeration. Excavations by the steamy gulf, in hilly Yemen, and among the stony flatlands to the south of Jordan push the peninsula's history much further into the past and, except in the vast dune area of the Empty Quarter, reveal considerable achievements in state-building, engineering, and agriculture. Long before the Christian era, great kingdoms rose on the north shores of the Indian Ocean: the queen of Sheba who visited Solomon, for example, almost certainly ruled in southern Arabia, not Ethiopia; and the ruins of the vast dam built by the Himyarite kings at Marib in Yemen during the lifetime of the Roman empire still impress us today, some fifteen centuries after its destruction. Pre-Islamic literature has long enjoyed high esteem among those who read it in the original or in translation, and inscriptions abound in a script that is the precursor of modern Arabic. Yet the ignorance of which the Arabs speak involves none of these things. It involves religious truth: in particular, knowledge of the One God, accepted in roughly similar terms by Jews, Christians, and, since the Prophet, by Muslims too.

According to Islam—that "submission to God" which binds in one brotherhood a series of contiguous societies from Morocco in the west to Indonesia in the east—Arabians had worshiped the Uncreated Creator at the Kaaba both before the Deluge and after it. By the seventh century the tribesmen of Arabia had relapsed into an idolatry that vitiated all actions and values. Unlike the Jews of the Diaspora with their Torah, or the

subjects of the Byzantine emperor with their Gospel, these tribesmen lacked a written revelation or scripture and hence any clear view of man's duties in this world and destiny in the next. To rectify this situation, Muslims believe, God sent the angelic messenger—who had announced the coming birth of Jesus to Mary—to deliver to Muhammad the first of a series of revelations that were collected, after his death, in a book known as the Noble Koran. The recipient of these revelations was a forty-year-old merchant whose father's name, Abdullah, "the slave of Allah," suggests a close tie to the chief god of the Koraysh, Mecca's dominant clan.

Setting aside the obvious differences in climate and geography, there is an affinity between Arabia's Age of Ignorance and the so-called Norse period in Europe's history. Arabian paganism, like Scandinavia's Age of Saga, contained elements so harsh as to affright more enlightened generations. Later hearers of Muhammad's revelations were particularly shocked, for instance, by the repeated mention of a crude method of population control in pre-Muslim Arabia: the live burial of girl babies. On the Day of Judgment, says the Koran, "the female infant, buried alive, will be questioned, for what crime was she killed?" Nobility nevertheless co-existed with savagery during the Age of Ignorance. The pagan way of life represented the efforts of men without a highly developed system of thought to come to terms with the stringent conditions imposed by the desert—and, at the same time, to maintain values they esteemed. These values owed their being to the hardships from which they sprang—and this very factor made them values that could wither in softer climes.

Unconditional hospitality was one rule of the desert,

and to this day generosity is the quality Arabs most admire. The ideal sprang from a practical recognition by nomads—and nomads accounted for four-fifths of the Hijaz's population—that the time could well come when survival would depend on a stranger's providing water and shade. Thus, no matter what sins a guest might have committed—including, perhaps, the murder of his host's closest kinsman—he would be made unquestioningly welcome and after three days would leave his host's tent with blessings and provisions. This rule endures legendary inflation in the story of Hatem the Generous, a youth who slaughtered his father's entire herd in honor of some chance visitors.

A degree of personal freedom inconceivable in societies based on agriculture was another characteristic engendered by Bedouin conditions. The tribal elders, or sheikhs, who exerted what authority existed in the desert, could hardly limit a tribesman's freedom, since if piqued or provoked he could always mount his camel and ride off, hiring out his services as herdsman or freelance warrior in some other region. The Bedouin themselves summed up the qualities they admired in the word *murū'ah*—the equivalent of the Latin *virtus,* since both words carry the meaning of "what fits a man." Yet the Arabian ideal of manly behavior was far from the swaggering machismo of some societies. The virtue included its own restraints and its own graces. Actions that offended against it aroused both external disapproval and a sense of shame in the offending individual. What *was to be* done strongly influenced what *was* done. Among other things, Arabian manliness did not imply the suppression of women, who enjoyed considerable independence. They could choose and dis-

miss their lovers; and when Arabs married it was the husband who generally took up residence with the wife, not vice versa. Women were also prominently engaged in business ventures. Witness Muhammad himself, an orphaned member of his tribe who owed his material advancement to the fact that he won the approval of a businesswoman, Khadijah. Fifteen years his senior, she chose him first as factor, then as husband. On occasion women even took part in tribal combats.

This society's defects, then, like its virtues, sprang from its circumstances. The Arabians lacked a generally shared philosophy or metaphysic. They saw life as a brief donation from a capricious fate, meaning that the best a human being could do was to seize the moment's pleasure and savor it to the full. Longing for the renown owed to courage or generosity came naturally to these people, to whom panache was second nature; but for the ego reflecting on its role in the cosmos, ultimate prospects were as bleak as they were inexplicable. Ideas of an afterlife were shadowy at best.

For Arabia's patchwork of clans, whose feuds concerned grazing rights and whose notion of glory was to emerge from these feuds, political unity seemed inconceivable. To make matters worse, the feuding Arabians had powerful neighbors: to the northwest, Byzantium; to the northeast, Persia; and, across the Straits of Mandab in Africa, Ethiopia. And these powers knew how to apply the age-old nostrum, "divide and rule," to Arab divisiveness. Moreover, the client kingdoms on the borders of Arabia often quarreled with one another over purely personal issues. Arabs did occasionally achieve power in their own right, however: one Roman emperor, Philip, actually was an Arab; and an Arab queen

Sixth-century Arabia was a crazy-quilt of tiny sheikhdoms, united by language but divided by recurrent quarrels over rights to water, pasturage, and key caravan routes. Blood feuds were endemic among the bellicose Bedouin (right), who had a strong sense of tribal, but no sense of national, identity. If Mecca was in any sense primus inter pares in those days, its hegemony was financial, not territorial. In 570, the year of Muhammad's birth, Yemeni soldiers advanced upon the thriving mercantile center. Their intention was to raze the Kaaba, but the reprisal raid failed. Legend attributes that failure to divine intervention; historians, to an epidemic of smallpox that swept through the Yemenite army as it neared Mecca.

ruled a kingdom based on Palmyra with the aid of Roman mercenaries. But such exceptions were rare, and strife was common.

In this general disunity, modified only by a common language and a shared, barren landscape, Mecca never achieved territorial control over much more than its immediate neighborhood. Its mercantile rulers, accepting this limitation, used their geographical position and their possession of the Kaaba to establish financial hegemony. Writing and mathematics flourished in the service of trade; caravans were taxed, wealth was amassed, outside labor was bought or hired; and Mecca's elite, the tribe of Koraysh, began to enjoy special prestige in the rest of Arabia. Mecca did not in fact require that centrality of control which, in other countries, has been the prerequisite of national defense; its isolation preserved the Hijaz from outside domination. The one serious attempt to subjugate Arabia from the west—by Aelius Gellus in the reign of Augustus—was prompted by the hope of securing its spice trade. That attempt failed. Another invasion took place in the period immediately before the advent of Islam—according to tradition, in the very year of Muhammad's birth. In A.D. 570, later dubbed the Year of the Elephant, Abraha, the Ethiopian king of Yemen, advanced north with the intention of leveling the Kaaba in revenge for a Meccan defilement of his large church at Sanaa. Legend has it that the invasion was defeated by divine intervention: the king's elephant stubbornly refused to march on the sacred shrine, and as the Ethiopians retreated a flock of birds pelted them with pebbles. From traditional descriptions of the septic pustules that erupted on the skins of the pelted soldiers, it seems likely that the actu-

al cause of the Ethiopians' defeat was an epidemic of smallpox. Disease was later to prove a recurrent danger to visitors to Mecca.

According to histories written after Muhammad's triumph, his grandfather Abdul Muttalib was the head man in Mecca during the Year of the Elephant. His power, whatever it was, cannot have been the equivalent of that of the Venetian doge, since Mecca was effectively governed by an assembly of elders. The Meccans used the money they amassed from trade to hire mercenaries; they also used slave-soldiers, although when put to it they played an active role as fighters themselves. For although it was essentially urban, the metropolis whose mansions pressed round the Kaaba, and whose smaller houses climbed the congested hillsides beyond, never lost its links with the desert hinterland. One custom in particular maintained these links: infants of the urban rich were boarded out with Bedouin women, who, for a fee, suckled and reared the children from the city alongside their own. This custom had valuable effects. It removed the young from an unhealthy dust bowl and enabled them to spend their formative years in the clear climate of the uplands. And the vigorous Bedouin way of life, coupled with a diet based on dates, bread, and camel's milk, stimulated physical endurance.

The urban child was thus temporarily enmeshed in desert society, and he came to regard his foster-brother as a cherished kinsman. In return, the nomadic tribe was emotionally linked to a Meccan family. And, most important of all, this practice forged links between each Meccan generation and the peninsula's basic culture. In addition to such skills as swordplay and riding, this cul-

وبكل النفس والجمالة والنفس والدابة انها ضغنت علي بالله فاضاعت نفص منرجها

ونشد مزرجها فلما دانني وزنت بالرقعة درهما وقطعة وقلت لها ارغبن في المشوف المعلم

واشرن الجي الدرهم فوجي بالسر المنهم وان اين ان نرجي فخذي القطعة واسرجن

نان الجي استخلاض البدر الثم والابلج الهمر وقالت دع جدالك ونلع عما بد الك فاسطه

طلع النشج ولبنه والسغر وباسج برذه فقالت ان النشج من اهل سروج وهو الذي ونثن

ture placed great emphasis on the word. As historian Philip Hitti has written, "No people in the world, perhaps, manifest such enthusiastic admiration for literary expression and are so moved by the word, spoken or written, as the Arabs." Eloquence was as much an attribute of the desert noble as courage or generosity. At an annual fair, held halfway between Mecca and Ta'if in the pilgrimage season, nomad poets hurled satirical verses at enemy tribes or extolled their own virtues as warriors or lovers. Poets were believed to be inspired by *jinns,* spirits akin to the demons from which Socrates claimed to draw inspiration. (To this day a madman is described by the Arabs as *majnun,* or *jinn*-possessed.) It was a society that rejoiced as much in the discovery of a new poet as in the birth of a son or foaling of a mare.

Boyhood exposure to desert life helped the men of Mecca to bridge the chasm between the financial obsessions of the city and the nomadic ideal. While the Meccans counted and traded, the Bedouin raided and rode. The Bedouin *ghazū,* or raid, as stylized as a dance, was carefully adapted to an economy so precarious that the heavy warfare of agrarian societies could have destroyed it. The *ghazū* was an affray in which shouting played as large a role as slashing and cutting. Its cattle-rustling triumphs were evanescent, for today's victor often became tomorrow's victim as the tribe he had robbed launched its counterattack. In time the Arabs were to reduce much of this violence to an exchange of oaths; serious damage was ordinarily limited by an elaborate system of fines in which payment of blood-money to a dead man's tribe discouraged vendettas.

If Mecca's position and wealth made it something of a desert Venice, its possession of a major shrine, as well as its proximity to others, gave it some of the aspects of a desert Delphi. The Kaaba was only one of a constellation of desert sanctuaries. A goddess known as al-'Uzza, "the Mightiest," who can probably be identified with Venus, although her cult was associated with human sacrifice, brooded over a trio of trees just east of Mecca. North of Mecca, halfway to the third Hijaz city of Yathrib, or Medina, a goddess similar in some respects to the Romans' Fortuna was represented by yet another black stone. A third, al-Lat, a daughter of Allah, was honored at Ta'if. But the Kaaba's role as the shrine of the dominant Koraysh won it increasing preeminence. Pilgrimages in honor of the god of the Kaaba and of two other deities, Isāf and Nāila (possibly corrupt forms of the Egyptian Osiris and Isis), had two advantages for a city like Mecca. The obvious one was the congenital readiness of the pilgrims to part with their money. The second, no less important, was the pilgrims' abstention from fighting during four months of the lunar year. One taboo month, Rajab, was taken up with rites peculiarly Meccan: devotees ran between the two hillocks of Shafa, where stood the statues of Isāf and Nāila, and Marwa. Three consecutive lunar months were needed to protect the major pilgrimage to the Kaaba, when visitors from afar came to take part in the ceremonies.

To ensure that these two pilgrimages occurred in the spring and autumn, thus saving pagan pilgrims from the arduous ordeal of an Islamic *hajj* undertaken during the scorching Arabian summer, extra days were periodically inserted in the lunar year—an ancient practice that allowed the faithful to adhere to the errant lunar calendar. The pagan rites themselves are nowhere precisely described. They probably involved circumambu-

For both good and ill, the culture of the desert has been shaped by the desert itself. Like the arid expanses of the Empty Quarter, Arabian culture is at once formidable and fragile, quick to spring to life and even quicker to fade away. By the dawn of the Christian era, when the plaque at right was carved, the tribes of the region had settled into permanent communities—all except the Bedouin, who were condemned by the vagaries of desert climate to a nomadic existence, dependent upon camels for transportation (right) and camel's-hair tents for shelter (left). For most of these tribesmen, life was to change very little in the next six centuries, and their ancient traditions and colorful language were to have a profound impact on the young Muhammad.

lation of the Kaaba and the kissing of the Black Stone and seem to have been conducted in a state of nudity.

A major problem for scholars is who precisely the god of the Kaaba was. Many have identified him with Allah and have claimed that this name is a contraction of *al-ilah,* meaning "the god." (In the same way, al-Lat would be a contraction of *al-ilaha,* "the goddess.") If this derivation is correct, it could have conveyed one of two meanings. To some Meccans, it may simply have meant their god, the god of their shrine. To others it may have carried the deeper significance that Allah was supreme among the many pagan gods in the same way that Zeus seemed supreme to the more reflective Greeks. Yet as in other pagan societies—or in societies where the cult of saints is widespread—the supreme god was often overlooked in favor of minor powers who seemed closer to the worshiper's aspirations.

Minor Arabian gods were usually represented by stones of significant shape or unusual material. As Mecca grew in importance, tribes from all over the peninsula imported their stones or fetishes to the Kaaba. The Kaaba's own tutelary god—thought by some to be the origin of Allah—was Hubal, whose statue had probably been imported from Iraq. Beside him stood arrows used for purpose of divination. Hubal was by no means the only representation of divinity in the shrine, however; a dove of aloes wood may have linked the Kaaba to the Arabian equivalent of Venus. Because the gods numbered exactly three hundred and sixty (and so corresponded to the days of the lunar year), and because the number seven figures prominently in Arabian rites (deriving from a time when there were thought to be seven planets), it has been argued that the religion of

the Kaaba involved an astral system with undertones of sun worship. If so, it formed part of a syncretic or composite cult typical of most types of pagan worship.

At the time of Muhammad's birth in A.D. 570 the Kaaba was a walled structure much lower than it is today and without a roof. And while Muhammad was still a youth a carelessly held incense lamp set the structure on fire. It was rebuilt with timbers from a Byzantine vessel providentially wrecked near Jiddah. The new building was roofed and a picture of the Virgin and Child was affixed to one of the supporting pillars. This intrusion of Christian iconography into pagan Arabia is not surprising and serves to illustrate the cultural influence of the great empire on Arabia's northwest border, since the early fourth century officially Christian. Notions and symbols deriving from Christianity—which took many eccentric forms in addition to the orthodoxy upheld by the Byzantine emperor—penetrated into Arabia at an early date. Some border statelets were actually converted, and deep inland, in the Hijaz and the central steppe, Christian ideas returned with the great trading caravans. In Egypt, Palestine, and Syria, rich Arabians were impressed by the splendid basilicas that represented the last flowering of Hellenistic architecture; the reflective were impressed by the hermitages, which served as desert retreats for men disgusted with the worldliness, cruelty, and factional squabbling of the Christianized empire.

Christianity was not the only form of monotheism known to pre-Islamic Arabians, however. After their defeat in two nationalistic revolts against Rome, the Jews had finally been expelled from Palestine by the Emperor Hadrian. Some exiles had migrated south into the

"O people, God commands you to make the Pilgrimage to this House so that He may reward you with Paradise and save you from the torment of Hell." Tradition ascribes this exhortation not to the Prophet but to his spiritual predecessor, Abraham, who is said to have erected the first House of God on the site now occupied by the Kaaba. This tale has obvious attractions for those who would engraft Islamic history to biblical myth, but its likelihood is refuted by the Bible itself, which locates Abraham in Canaan, far to the north. Indeed, as recently as the early Christian epoch the Kaaba was but one of dozens of pagan shrines dotting the Arabian landscape. As Mecca grew in commercial and cultural significance, however, so did the Kaaba; by the year of Muhammad's birth it housed 360 tutelary deities, gathered from every corner of the Island of the Arabs. This unusual view of the ancient, kiswa-draped shrine shows it as few hajjis ever see it, rising from the gleaming marble pavement that is normally thronged with the faithful.

30

No one has any way of knowing what the interior of the Kaaba looked like 1,300 years ago. Only a privileged few are admitted to its cramped inner chamber even today, and those who enjoyed that privilege in pagan times left no descriptions behind them. We know the space was crammed with idols, some from as far away as Iraq, and that its walls were festooned with arrows used in divination. And we suspect that its gloom was dispelled by mosque lamps not unlike the one at right. Its furnishings were certainly primitive, of that we can be sure: no match for Jerusalem's Second Temple, nor even for the Yemeni mosque that supplied the subject matter for the richly detailed, magnificently woven carpet shown at left.

northern Hijaz, and in the extended oasis of Yathrib, or Medina, 270 miles north of Mecca, they had established agricultural colonies among Arabians whose language was akin to their own. They continued to practice their ancient religion and, one may confidently assume, to explain it to those interested in such matters.

The monotheistic concepts of these two faiths, however distorted by heretical accretions or provincial ignorance, inspired and irritated the Arabians in equal measure. Their own polytheism, despite its manliness and stirring poetry, lacked the idyllic aspects that made the paganism of Egypt and Greece so attractive. Because the sandy soil of Arabia could not provide the surplus production that greener, richer countries translated into pictorial and sculptural art, the idols in the Arabian shrines were uncouth compared with the majestic statues that dominated the dim interiors of Egypt's temples or the personifications of nobler human qualities that illuminated Hellenic existence. Although, like Greece, Arabia lacked a despotic priesthood, the harshness of its daily life inhibited the kind of rational disputation that had developed into science in the coastal cities of the Aegean.

In a sense seventh-century Mecca resembled Delphi in function but not in cultural achievement or natural beauty. And the paganism of the Kaaba could not unify the Arabians as the Gospel united the Greeks or the Torah united the dispersed Jews. Nor could its semi-magical rites provide a convincing explanation of the universe and man's role in it. On the contrary, tribal attachment to rival fetishes facilitated the exploitation of Arabian disunity by interested outsiders. The Arabians had never been known to unite in defense of common

interests, let alone a common ideal. All the same, Byzantine and Jewish modes of thought were alien as well as challenging, and it irked Arabians to have to admit their metaphysical inferiority to men they despised. The survival of their primitive and mixed beliefs alongside more articulated systems produced a restlessness of spirit similar to that which had prepared the Roman empire for the acceptance of the Gospel.

Mecca in the last decades of the Age of Ignorance thus blended characteristics that were strikingly opposed. Politically, the city was in advance of the great autocracies on its frontiers. A small-scale republic, it was run with considerable subtlety by a plutocracy whose power was limited by the checks and balances of a tribal system. No Meccan with tribal affiliations was unprotected, as the career of Muhammad himself was to show. Yet the tribal power that restrained this financial oligarchy was the collective force of nomads, desert men who had produced no more complex response to the ultimate mysteries than a defiant shriek or stoic courage. At the same time these technologically and metaphysically backward nomads had the freshness and health that are the eternal antitheses of decadence. The sharp-eyed merchants and camel-drivers who had admired Byzantine palaces and churches had also descried the national restlessness of the Syrians and Egyptians, ruled by Greek masters from Constantinople. Behind its brocade, Byzantium was a divided and vulnerable society. The weakness of the New Rome became alarmingly evident early in the seventh century when a Persian army rampaged deep into Egypt, capturing Jerusalem en route and carrying off the most sacred relics of Christendom, including the True Cross,

discovered some centuries earlier by the mother of the
first Christian emperor. Arabians had traveled into Persia as well, and there, no less than in Byzantium, they
reported of inner weakness.

Proud of their manliness but aware of their lack of a
convincing metaphysic, thoughtful Arabians took different paths. Some, like the cousin of the woman who was
to marry Muhammad, embraced Christianity; others
opted for the sterner monotheism of the Hebrew
prophets; yet others sought indications that once, in
the mist of time, Arabians too had professed one creed.
Jewish visitors to Mecca—who entered freely, there being no taboo at this time on who entered the sacred
territory—may have first suggested to Meccans the notion that their Kaaba had associations with Ibrahim (the
biblical Abraham), whose son by Hagar, Ismail (or Ishmael), had fathered the Arabian branch of the Semitic
family. If this were true, the pagan rites revolving
round the Kaaba could acquire a deeper significance.
Such rereading of ancient customs and texts is a permanent function of the human mind; Islam was to give
the Kaaba a new role, and this significance was in turn
enlarged by later Muslims.

But even the most daring advocates of a new metaphysic could hardly have foreseen the revolutionary
manner in which the traditional ways of Arabia were to
be transformed. Only the word miracle can describe the
revolution's major achievement, the achievement without which all other achievements were impossible—the
brief welding of all Arabia in one missionary purpose.

At this same time Bedouin values were to receive a
decisive jolt. In their pure form they would survive only
among those too isolated or too poor to integrate
themselves into the new framework. For Meccans and
most Arabians the society in which women had discarded their lovers by changing the direction of their tents
and in which men fought as freelance warriors was to
be exchanged for an empire that brought rewards to
the faithful in this world and heavenly consolations in
the next. In place of the desert *majlis,* or counsel tent,
where a barefoot tribesman addressed his sheikh face
to face, would rise the marbled palace where the postulant prostrated himself to power. The love affairs of
such wandering poets as Imr al-Qais were to be proscribed while men plump as castrated cats guarded vast
boarding schools of idle women. And instead of snatching the fragile joys of this life with a clear conscience,
Arabians were to tread a knife-edge between a fire
where

> as often as their skins are roasted through,
> We shall change them for fresh skins, that
> they may taste the penalty . . .

and a Paradise entertaining the believers

> on thrones encrusted, reclining on them, facing
> each other; youths of perpetual freshness will
> circumambulate them; with goblets, beakers, and
> cups of clear-flowing fountains: no hangover will
> they receive therefrom, nor will they suffer
> intoxication: and with fruits, any they may
> choose; and fowl-flesh as they may desire; and
> *houris* like well-guarded pearls; a reward for
> what they have done.

33

III

The Messenger of God

Unlike Abraham, Moses, or Jesus, the Prophet of Mecca lived his adult life in the glare of history. An idea, backed by arms, established Muhammad, in the last decade of his life, as the leader and legislator of a small but expansionist state. By that time he was already in diplomatic touch with the empires his followers were to defeat. And by that time he had known triumphs—and troubles—experienced by few other religious innovators. Yet even with a figure as historical as Muhammad we are unable to date precisely all the events of his career. Mecca, however important it may have been inside Arabia, was on the fringe of the world that kept accurate annals, and by the time the first Muslim biographers took up their pens in the eighth century of the Christian era they felt such reverence for Muhammad as God's final envoy that they inevitably included coincidences that appealed to them and marvels of the kind associated with earlier prophets.

The temptation to link God's irruption into Arabian history with the Yemeni-Ethiopian assault on Mecca proved irresistible to these biographers—which is why tradition puts Muhammad's birth as A.D. 570, the so-called Year of the Elephant. He may actually have been born a few years later—there is no means of knowing for certain—but we may have confidence in the main facts recorded about his family situation, even if some details are incorrect. His father, who died before Muhammad's birth, remains a shadowy figure. His traditional name—Abdullah, slave of Allah—probably implies a link with the Kaaba's pagan cult, not the One God. And Abdullah is conceivably a pious addition; he may well have borne, like most of his contemporaries, a pagan name. What matters is that Muhammad himself was a posthumous child, born to a widow in a society where tribal and family relationships were all-important. Muhammad was thus a deprived member of the ruling family, the Koraysh. Without committing ourselves overmuch to the teachings of Freud, we may see in the young Muhammad's lack of an earthly father a factor predisposing him to search for a heavenly substitute. His mother, Amina, apparently had some family link with Yathrib, or Medina. This could have had a significant bearing on her son's later decision to make that city his headquarters, even though Amina herself died when Muhammad was six and apparently played little role even in his infancy. One of the Bedouin women who came to Mecca looking for children to raise in the desert took on the penniless orphan—according to one tradition, through an intuitive awareness of his shining future. What matters is that Amina's consent to this desert upbringing enabled Muhammad to acquire a respectful familiarity with nomadic values and a sensitivity to the rich Arab vocabulary that never left him.

Although Islam preserves no relic so intimately linked to Muhammad as the Shroud of Turin is to Jesus, the literary tradition regarding his appearance is much fuller. The Gospels tell us nothing directly of what Jesus looked like, and the early traditions disagree. Islamic tradition, on the contrary, preserves a description of Muhammad's build and mannerisms that is not disputed. Stocky, probably a little above average height, he was a man whose every movement gave the impression of immense energy. He walked fast, as though pacing downhill, taxing the friends who tried to keep up with him; and when he turned he moved his whole trunk, not merely his head. His large forehead, prominent hooked nose, black, lustrous eyes flecked with brown, and fair complexion all conformed with Arabian ideals of male good looks. His speech was economical, rapid, and to the point. Good with children, he also had a sympathy for animals uncharacteristic of his time and place (on one campaign he was to station soldiers over a bitch, lest her puppies be disturbed by men on the march). His youthful nickname—al-Amin, the Reliable—shows a serious cast of character that probably recommended Muhammad to the Korayshi businesswoman Khadijah, who advanced his career. Around forty, and fifteen years older than he, she made Muhammad her business agent, then married him. The marriage was providential. A much-quoted passage of the Koran—whose source material for the Prophet's life, though meager, is at least contemporary—calls attention to those of God's bounties lavished on Muhammad personally. "Did he not find you an orphan and give you shelter?" it begins. In actuality, the boy had been looked after first by his grandfather, Abdul Muttalib, and then by his paternal uncle, Abu Taleb, who defended him against his enemies, even though he never accepted his nephew's religion.

"And he found you wandering, and he gave you guidance. And he found you in need and he enriched you," the Koran continues. The last expression by no means implies that Muhammad's wealth was even a hundredth of that possessed by later Caliphs—he darned his own clothes and ate a simple diet—but it indicates that his career was not hampered by the need to earn a living or clamped in the duress of a rich male patron. The word "wandering" in this passage leads us to believe that in his youth Muhammad was as pagan as other Meccans. But if he performed, as is likely, the same idolatrous ceremonies as his peers, it is probable that even then he brooded on the symbolism behind the rituals.

Khadijah bore Muhammad sons, all of whom died in infancy. Of his four daughters, only Fatimah, whom he married to his cousin Ali, the son of Abu Taleb, gave Muhammad and Khadijah descendants.

In the crisis that was to overwhelm Muhammad toward middle life—and, eventually, deliver him from pagan error—Khadijah was to provide moral support that far outweighed what she had given Muhammad before in terms of security and money. The crisis, by its very nature, remains clouded in mystery. Even those thinkers who bequeath a detritus of papers to memorial libraries rarely clarify the stages of their mental growth, and sudden leaps of the mind are much harder to record. In the case of Muhammad's spiritual development there is no such documentation, and a lack of dates makes the task of analyzing what happened extremely hazardous. For one thing, there is even some dispute as to whether he could read and write. An adjective applied to him in the Koran—*ummi*, which can mean national, native, or illiterate—has been used in the last sense by hagiographers. If Muhammad was ignorant of the alphabet, it is implied, this would throw into greater relief the eloquence of his revelations and emphasize their independence from his cerebral processes. More probably, the word means that he was unversed in the written texts of the Old and New Testaments. And in this connection it is significant that, while the Koran tells and retells stories of the patriarchs and preaching prophets, it ignores Hebrew seers who used the pen.

Muhammad is in many ways the most human—and in all ways the most modern—of great religious leaders. Too human, in fact, for conventional sainthood; and too modern to be consumed whole by legend. Indeed, for all his obvious talents—and despite his astonishing achievements—Muhammad remains resolutely human: capable of lust, indecision, passion, and error. The first four decades were in no way remarkable, for Muhammad was forty before he received his first divine revelations in a cave on Mount Hira (top right), which is still visited by Muslim pilgrims. In their early phase Muhammad's teachings met with considerable resistance, for attempts at conversion often angered non-believers (opposite). As Muhammad's influence grew, so, inevitably, did the apocrypha surrounding his life. One of these tales is the subject of the exquisite miniature at lower right.

36

In fact, as a Meccan and as the employee of a businesswoman, Muhammad had probably learned the rudiments of writing and arithmetic. But foreign ideas more puzzling than accounts were current in Mecca. Arabians seeking answers to the larger metaphysical questions that monotheism claimed to answer did so by meditation, fasting, and praying. One of these was a member of Muhammad's immediate family—Khadijah's elderly cousin, Waraqah ibn Nawfal, who became a Christian. Around his fortieth year, Muhammad joined such questing individuals. Perplexed by the failure of the Arabian tradition to give justice a spiritual basis or to explain man's place in the cosmos, he took to frequenting a cave on Mount Hira, one of the dry hills ringing Mecca. There he indulged in bouts of meditation. Such strenuous thought, in torrid heat and coupled with abstinence from food, may well have precipitated an eruption of his unconscious. Similar experiences have been documented in other centuries and other cultures, and the inspiration has not always been deemed divine. A famous instance of the latter is *Kubla Khan,* Samuel Taylor Coleridge's mesmeric fragment, which combines, like leaves fallen into a deep well, details from his recent reading fused into a mysterious vision by the effects of opium and then silenced by the arrival of an unnamed stranger. In Muhammad's case, some unknown factor induced a psychic storm that both terrified him and left him reciting an audible command.

There are two theories as to the content of this first communication from heaven. One identifies it with the exhortation to Muhammad, "wrapped up in a mantle," to arise and warn. Another identifies it with the command to "recite in the name of your Lord who created:

created man from a clot." Traditions set down long after the event disagree as to whether Muhammad's consciousness of an inner command was accompanied by a vision of God himself or of the Angel Gabriel. The former hypothesis may be the more likely, as the earliest references to Gabriel in Muhammad's revelations do not occur in the first ten years of his mission.

Such disputes hardly matter, either to the devout or to the reader. What is clear is that, sometime around A.D. 610, Muhammad received the first of a series of revelations that were to be continually augmented over the next two decades. After his death, the revelations were collected in the volume, of roughly New Testament length, the world knows as the Koran. Since the word Koran probably derives from the Syriac *qiryana,* meaning a scriptural recitation, it would accord with the second of the two suggested initial revelations, which begins with the Arabic imperative *iqraa',* close in both sound and meaning to the Syriac noun. The story that Muhammad, in his alarm and bewilderment at the revelations, was tempted to kill himself, also rings true. Luckily, in his inner turmoil he turned to Khadijah, who was convinced that his experience could only come from God, not Satan, and fetched her Christian cousin, Waraqah. The old man urged Muhammad to rejoice, saying that he had been visited by the same *namūs* as had previously descended on Moses and Jesus. (The word *namūs* is in itself an interesting instance of the interdependence of cultures. It derives from *nomos,* the Greek word for law, which, in New Testament times, was used both for the Christian revelation and for the sacred books of Jewish scripture.)

The revelations that came to Muhammad were some-

times short and pithy, sometimes discursive; dry as Leviticus or poetic as Revelation. Muslim scholars have divided the Koran's 114 *surahs,* or chapters, into those revealed at Mecca, during the first phase of Muhammad's prophethood, and those revealed at Medina in the second. The shorter, ecstatic, Meccan chapters tend to be preoccupied with a double vision of God's beneficence and the catastrophe menacing those who reject him. The longer, Medinan chapters are mostly given over to legislating for the needs and duties of the Islamic community. Yet the divisions are not rigid. There is, for example, a sublime passage about the nature of God, almost impossible to render in adequate English, that interrupts a chapter dealing with rules governing the dress, comportment, and divorce of women.

God is the light of the heavens and the earth
His light may be compared to a niche
Within it a lamp
And the lamp in glass
And the glass like a blazing planet
It is lit from a blessed tree
An olive neither of the east
Nor of the west
Its oil is all but luminous
Though fire scarce touched it
Light upon light

In announcing the will of this luminous deity, Muhammad had reason to fear the ridicule of his countrymen. They naturally assumed that, like a poet or soothsayer, he was publicizing his own compositions. They were phrased not in the strict verse forms of tra-

dition but in a kind of loose, rhyming prose, prompting his critics to belittle them for not excelling in a medium they in fact avoided. Like the odes of tribal poets, the revelations were attributed by these critics to a *jinn,* or demonic familiar. Muhammad himself was accused of being *majnun,* demon-possessed. The new Prophet was unable to laugh off these charges; they were too dangerous. The trust of the few who accepted Muhammad as a divine messenger, like his own confidence in himself and his mission, was narrowly balanced on the belief that his revelations differed in kind from mere love poems or satires.

The word the Koran uses to describe this supernatural authority is *wahy,* which the Koranic scholar Richard Bell has defined as "the communication of an idea by some quick suggestion or prompting; by, as we might say, a flash of inspiration." The Koran by no means limits the experience of *wahy* to Muhammad: Noah is prompted in the same language to build his ark; and the bee is prompted to take up her abode in hills, trees, and the arbors men put up. Later, Muhammad's revelations were further defined as emanating from a preexisting book, of which he received an Arabic version. And Muslim theologians have since defined the Koran as "the speech of Allah, written in the copies, preserved in the memories, recited by the tongues, revealed to the Prophet. Our pronouncing, writing and reciting the Koran is created, whereas the Koran itself is uncreated." The charge that Muhammad had simply *composed* his revelations, rather than *receiving* them, was thus a greater peril to the Prophet than death in battle. The latter would be a personal calamity; the former, a catastrophe for all Islam. This helps to explain why a man

بسم الله الرحمن الرحيم

الحمد لله رب العالمين ۞ الرحمن الرحيم

مالك يوم الدين ۞ اياك نعبد واياك

نستعين ۞ اهدنا الصراط المستقيم

صراط الذين انعمت عليهم غير

المغضوب عليهم ولا الضالين

مكية وهي سبع ايات

usually thought of as forgiving and merciful was prepared to sanction the killing of several poets who dared to ridicule his claims.

Not surprisingly, in the centuries when Christendom faced its greatest challenge, first from Muhammad's Arabian and then from his Turkish disciples, Christian polemicists hurled similar charges against the enemy Prophet. It was left to a dour nineteenth-century Scot, Thomas Carlyle, writing *On Heroes, Hero-Worship, and the Heroic in History,* to postulate Muhammad's personal sincerity. Subsequent writers have generally conceded this quality—which does not, of course, imply that such distinguished writers on Muhammad as Montgomery Watt (a Church of Scotland minister) and Maxime Rodinson (a Marxist of Jewish origin) accepted Muhammad's theological claims. Had they done so, they would presumably have become Muslims. What they do accept is that his life can be adequately explained only if Muhammad's belief that his revelations came from God is accepted as sincere.

Muhammad's vision of God was of a being not only beneficent but transcendent, and one short chapter sums up the total monotheism that is distinctive of the Koran. Its Arabic title, *Ikhlas,* carries the meaning "purification of the soul from all but God":

Say: He is God unique
God the absolute
He begets not and is not begotten
And there is no one like unto him.

In summoning his fellow Meccans to this God's exclusive worship, Muhammad did not consider that he was inventing a new religion. On the contrary, he believed he was restating perennial monotheism in Arabian terms. The Koran applies Muslim, a term for one who has "submitted," to those monotheists of the past who had accepted the notion that this One God created and sustained the cosmos, revealing knowledge of himself to a chain of prophets beginning with Abraham (or Ibrahim) and ending with Jesus. The inclusion of Jesus as a Muslim prophet may surprise some Christians, although one Gospel account describes him as a prophet in its account of the entry into Jerusalem. The lines quoted from the Koran clearly exclude any literal belief in the Incarnation; yet at the same time, as historian Geoffrey Parrinder has pointed out, Jesus receives more honorable titles in the Koran than any other figure of the past. These include, along with Prophet and Messiah, Messenger, Servant, Word, and Spirit of God. Mary, the only woman the Koran calls by her proper name, is in fact mentioned more times in the Islamic scripture than in the New Testament.

Muhammad's burning monotheism naturally worried those Meccans who earned their living from religious tourism. Their hostility differed little from that which St. Paul had encountered six centuries earlier from the silversmiths of Ephesus, who found that sales of statuettes of the city's remarkable many-breasted Diana declined after Paul's preaching. Arabian nationalism was probably also offended at the manner in which Muhammad's converts, largely recruited from the poor, had adopted a non-Arabian retinue of prophets and taken to prostrating themselves in prayer toward Jerusalem, a city under Byzantine control. St. Paul had suffered similar hostility from fellow Jews who resented his open-

Milestones similar to the one at left above now mark the road from Mecca to Medina—little more than a dusty footpath when Muhammad and his followers fled north from inhospitable Mecca in 622, Year One of the Muslim calendar. The mosques that the Prophet himself founded at this time (left, below), like al-Quba, the first mosque erected in Medina, were simple, whitewashed structures made of wattle and clay. The sprawling Prophet's Mosque (above), which dominates the center of Medina, is a later and far more elaborate edifice. An architectural amalgam, it combines Ottoman arcades (rear) with polished marble pillars (foreground) that were put up in this century. Muslims believe that all prayers uttered in this sanctuary have one thousand times the efficacy of those offered anywhere else—except, of course, those spoken within the precincts of the Sacred Mosque in Mecca during the season of the hajj, which have concomitant value.

43

At first Muhammad hoped to persuade Arabia's other monotheists, the Jews and the Christians, to convert to Islam—which he saw not as a new, and perforce antagonistic, creed but as a recasting of perennial monotheism in purely Arabian terms. Superficially, at least, this affiliation made sense—and so Muhammad made a determined effort at peaceful persuasion. The manuscript detail at near left, for example, shows a rabbi reading the section of the Bible in which Muhammad's coming is predicted. And, below left, a group of monks discuss Islam. Jews and Christians, however, were ultimately unmoved by Muslim teachings.

ness to the Gentiles. But Muhammad was not to suffer physical persecution of the sort that, in Paul's case, culminated in decapitation under Nero. Indeed, the sufferings of Muhammad and his early converts have probably been exaggerated from pious motives, for whatever the pagans might have liked to do, Muhammad's connections with the powerful Koraysh protected him and most of his followers from imprisonment, torture, or death. Even so, he found it expedient to send some of his followers into exile across the Red Sea in Abyssinia. There the Muslims were interrogated by the Ethiopian Emperor Negus on their attitude to Jesus. Their reply was to recite the chapter on Mary, which indicated the high respect in which the Koran held Jesus and his mother.

The persecutions in Mecca have been cited in tradition as the factor precipitating Muhammad's most radical move: the decision to send his converts ahead to Medina, where he would then join them. This "migration," or abandonment of his birthplace, took place in September 622, a date later fixed as Year One of the Islamic era. Even at the time the Meccans sensed potential menace in the migration, and Muhammad and his friend Abu Bakr, the last to leave, were hotly pursued. They escaped by hiding in a cave with a narrow entrance. According to legend, a spider swiftly spun a web over the entrance, and this convinced the pursuers that it had long been untenanted.

In reality, a number of other elements were involved in the decision to migrate, first among them the fact that the impetus of Muhammad's religious movement had begun to flag. An attempt to win over the people of Ta'if, much nearer to Mecca than Medina, had met with rebuff, for example. But it was, in all probability, two personal losses that actually tipped the balance. First, Muhammad's uncle, Abu Taleb, died, depriving him of his political support with the Koraysh. Khadijah's death shortly thereafter left the Prophet emotionally bereft. The notion of going to Medina was probably mooted to him by Medinan pilgrims to the Kaaba. They had been attracted by his preaching and recognized in him a potential leader for their northern oasis, only then recovering from a disastrous war. The presence of Muhammad and his followers would reinforce their fortunes.

Medina presented a total contrast to arid Mecca. Spread out on an upland plateau situated above a copious reservoir of water, it was an archipelago of fertile patches protected not by one encircling wall but by village fortresses. Its rich soil produced a variety of fruits, particularly date palms. Its greater proximity to the Mediterranean was also important. A number of Jewish tribes, either the descendants of Jewish emigrants from Palestine or converts, were engaged in agriculture in the region. In theory, they could widen the Prophet's knowledge of the scriptures; in fact, he probably hoped to win them to acceptance of his prophethood. The Byzantine frontier, in what is now southern Jordan, was not far to the north, which put Christian influence much closer than at Mecca. Yet one of Muhammad's initial discoveries, upon arriving in Medina, was how little the earlier monotheists agreed. The Jews rejected the notion that Jesus had been their Messiah, while the Christians, at odds with the Jews, were themselves split into many sects.

Medina was to reveal new aspects of Muhammad's genius. The visionary became a man of action who, in his last ten years, turned the oasis into the powerhouse of a united Arabia. His situation imposed the need to act; his skills made the action uniquely successful. Among other things he was responsible for the emigrants, who, in abandoning Mecca, had also abandoned their means of livelihood. The way Muhammad chose to feed them was by plundering the rich caravans that passed within striking distance of Medina on their way to Mecca. These attacks could be justified as chastening the idolaters and compelling them to accept the truth of his vision—but persuading Medina's settled Arabs to countenance such dangers was a real achievement. The helpers, the term by which the Medinans were distinguished from the emigrants, can hardly have bargained for so combative a leader. A first, small-scale venture was followed by the symbolically important battle of Badr. Both were successful, and the helpers acquiesced; but when these victories were followed by reverses, they began to grumble. (The Koran uses the term *munafiqīn*, two-faced or hypocritical, for such lukewarm adherents.) Sterner condemnation was to be the lot of the Jews, for contrary to Muhammad's hopes, they rejected his claim to be a Prophet and ridiculed his interpretation of the scriptures. Challenged by a threat graver than the cowardice or opportunism of the *munafiqīn*, Muhammad took a series of steps to break with these unassimilable monotheists.

In Year One of the Hejira, or Migration, Muhammad had appointed the tenth of the Arabic month of Muharram as a day of fasting. The resemblances to the Jewish Day of Atonement were evident. In Year Two, the voice of *wahy* proclaimed: "The month of Ramadan is that in

which the Koran was sent down as a guide to people. So every one of you who is present [i.e., not absent from home on a journey] during that month should spend it in fasting; but if anyone is ill, or on a journey, he should make up the prescribed period with the missed number of days later."

Ramadan was to introduce a mode of fasting peculiar to Islam. For an entire month the daylight hours were a period of drastic abstinence: from the moment, before dawn, when a white thread could first be distinguished from a black, until sunset, all adult Muslims had to abstain from food, drink, and sex. Such a fast could, of course, be lethal in an Arctic summer, where the sun does not sink at all; it simply could not be observed in a sunless and Arctic winter. In Muhammad's own climate, the vagaries of the lunar calendar meant that Ramadan occasionally came in summer when it could be almost unendurable. Apologists in the Muslim press nowadays claim that such fasting is physically beneficial but non-Muslim physicians are not known to commend it. In truth, the poor, who need to labor, suffer greater hardship during Ramadan than the rich, who can sleep through the daylight hours.

Without apparent concern for such considerations, the Koran instituted the fast as a religious discipline. Like many of the regulations codified for Jews by Ezra, it had the effect, probably intentional, of separating the Muslim "nation" from outsiders—and so strengthened its cohesion. Yet, surprisingly, this month, in so many ways, is also the Muslim season equivalent to Christmas. After the evening breakfast the nights are spent in innocent diversion and family visits. Storytellers enthrall crowds in the brightly lit mosques and markets,

and most Muslims, when asked whether they like Ramadan, reply without hesitation, "Of course!"

Year Two of the Migration signaled yet another break with the Jews. This came in the revelation that the Kaaba in Mecca, not the city of Jerusalem, was the *kiblah,* or focus for Muslim prayer. Muslims were also enjoined to make the pilgrimage to Mecca. For a few years this command was impracticable, the idolaters still controlling access to the Kaaba and Mecca as a whole. Alcohol was also proscribed at around this time, and several considerations commended this prohibition. The Bedouin, on whom history had thrust dramatic responsibilities, were a people of extremes; moderation was not their characteristic virtue. They could either abstain totally, or get drunk. In pagan days, they got drunk. In Mecca, close to Zemzem, the well water was fermented with dates to make a fiery brew, and prayer after such potations could soon degenerate. The richer Arabians knew of wine, but only as a luxury, for Jews and Christians enjoyed a monopoly on its sale.

These moves toward religious independence were accompanied by the progressive elimination of the Jews, first from Medina, and then from the entire Hijaz. In the aftermath of the first raid at Nakhlah, a Jewish tribe was coerced into migrating north toward Transjordan. In Year Three, the Meccans attempted to punish the Muslims for their successes. Khalid ibn Walid, later recognized as Islam's greatest general, commanded a Meccan army that defeated the Muslims but made the political mistake of not occupying Medina. When he withdrew, the resilient Muslims of Medina promptly laid siege to a second Jewish tribe in their fortress.

Tranquil and untrammelled today, its looks belie its role in history, for the oasis of Badr, which lies along the ancient caravan route from Mecca to Aleppo, was the site of one of the most critical confrontations in Muhammad's campaign to capture all Arabia for Islam. Here, in the third year of the Migration, his troops were to encounter—and eventually to rout—a vastly superior force of Meccan soldiers.

The years of the Hejira, or Migration, proved to be precarious ones for the Prophet and his disciples. Hard-pressed to deal with contention at home, they were ill-equipped to cope with aggressors from other lands, a category that eventually—some would say inevitably—included the Mongols of Central Asia, who are featured in this detail from a manuscript illumination dated 1314.

They, too, surrendered and were forced to travel north. In Year Five a much larger Meccan force—according to one account numbering as many as ten thousand warriors—besieged Medina with the active collaboration of this banished Jewish tribe.

By this time only one substantial Jewish group remained in Medina—the clan of Korayzah. The Korayzah were understandably hostile to Muhammad but probably confined their hostility to negotiations with his enemies. For their outward neutrality they were to pay dearly. The Meccans had been foiled in their assault on Medina by a hastily dug trench, an innovation in the art of war that they considered unsporting. Muhammad's previous shows of leniency were probably what persuaded the Korayzah to opt for the fate of the previous groups, all of whom had been allowed to leave. They accepted a suggestion from the Prophet that their fate should be decided by a judge chosen from an Arab tribe with whom they enjoyed traditions of friendship. The judge, himself wounded in the war and destined to die soon thereafter, made all present swear to accept his judgment. This done, he decreed that all the males (save a handful who converted) should be slain, and the women and children sold into slavery. The next day the male Jews (some figures give the number as six hundred, others as nine hundred) were decapitated in the marketplace. This harsh sentence served two purposes in Muhammad's statecraft. Besides eliminating a fifth column in his capital, the Arab tribes confederate to the Korayzah were taught the vivid lesson that henceforth loyalty to Islam transcended all other bonds, whether of family loyalty or tribal friendship.

The danger of further Jewish opposition was met anew in Year Seven, when the northern Jewish oasis of Khaybar was besieged and taken. On this occasion Muhammad introduced what was to become standard practice when Muslim rulers dealt with enemies who were at the same time "people of the Book," or monotheists. They were given the choice of conversion to Islam or of continuing to live and worship where they were, on payment of a tax. This policy, humane in the context of the time, was soon to introduce a conflict of interest. While their religion taught early Muslim rulers to aim for the conversion of as many souls as possible, their treasuries benefited from perpetuating a productive and tax-paying subject population. The Arabians also resented the notion that non-Arabians should enjoy equal status with themselves. On the other side, gifted converts, such as the Persians, were to come to resent their second-class status and to work for the overthrow of the dynasty that enforced it.

In these operations, designed to establish a unified and effective state, Muhammad never lost sight of Mecca. His birthplace remained his major territorial objective, and in Year Six he felt strong enough to move south with sacrificial animals, which he intended to slaughter at the *'umrah*, or minor pilgrimage (see Chapter 4). On this occasion the Meccans blocked his advance and secured a Pyrrhic victory. To prevent bloodshed, the Prophet agreed to sign a treaty which stated that the Muslims would advance no further that year but would have the right to come as pilgrims a year later. This concession was vitally important to Muhammad, for it implicitly recognized him as the leader of an Islamic state.

Muhammad consolidated his hold on Medina in Year Five of the Hejira by subduing the neutral clan of the Korayzah, Jews who surrendered to the Prophet in the expectation that their lives, like those of so many who opposed Muhammad, would be spared. Instead, the Prophet made the Korayzah the objects of a sanguinary lesson in loyalty—by ordering the execution of every male.

The Prophet, who by Year Six had cut a new stencil for his people, had at the same time cut a new pattern for himself. He was never to lose his simple manners or democratic accessibility, and his Medinan residence was in no sense a palace. Its construction had begun a few days after his arrival in September 622. After a brief pause at the edge of the oasis Muhammad had moved forward through the date palms. Since leading Medinans contended for the honor of having him as neighbor or guest, there may be truth in the tradition that Muhammad announced he would live where his camel halted. His house, now the site of Islam's second most holy mosque, became the modest headquarters of a nascent empire. It consisted of an open space, some fifty-six yards square and enclosed by a mud-brick wall ten feet high. On the south a portico of palm-bole columns supported a roof of palm fronds daubed with mud. Here, in addition to running his government, Muhammad led prayers and maintained a growing household. During Khadijah's life he had remained monogamous. The Koran had meanwhile revealed that, provided he treated them equally, a Muslim could marry four wives at one time. (Twentieth-century Muslims have taken this requirement as an implicit rejection of polygamy, given the impossibility of truly equal treatment.)

In the Prophet's case a somewhat complex revelation exempted him from the limits imposed on other male Muslims. After Khadijah's death he was to marry at least a dozen women. His considerable harem—a word akin to *haram,* though in this case the taboo relates to a man's women, not to territory—occupied small houses built to the east of the Prophet's enclosure but with access to his courtyard. An eyewitness who inspected these buildings just before they were demolished in A.D. 707 has left this description: "There were four houses of mud brick, with apartments partitioned off by palm branches plastered with mud and not divided into rooms. Over the doors were curtains of black haircloth. Each curtain measured three by three cubits [about 5' by 5']. One could touch the roof with the hand." Here the Prophet apparently visited his wives on a rota basis. Except for Sawdah, who had followed a first husband, now dead, to Abyssinia, all Muhammad's later wives were acquired after the Migration.

Human affections cannot be controlled by edict, however, and the Prophet's undoubted favorite was Abu Bakr's daughter, Ayesha. He married her in Year One of the Migration, having been betrothed to her three years earlier. Aged nine at the time of their marriage, she came to Muhammad's house still playing with her dolls. Father as much as husband, Muhammad joined in her childish games. Yet we would be wrong to picture Ayesha as an insipid child-wife of the sort Dickens was to depict thirteen centuries later. She could express an independent personality with irreverent wit and is the one person in the prophetic circle who seems to have spoken of Muhammad's revelations with an edge of humor. When the Voice revealed a marriage concession applicable only to the Prophet, according to a reliable tradition Ayesha said, "God is in haste to satisfy your desires." Muhammad showed her remarkable indulgence. Lagging behind on one expedition, she arrived late in Medina with a handsome nomad. Over a number of weeks Muhammad's enemies circulated scandals until a revelation crushingly silenced them and some of the scandal-mongers were flogged.

This intricately wrought brass and iron grille encloses
the south wall of the Prophet's tomb in Medina.
Burnished brass discs, set into the grille on either side
of the door, indicate to pilgrims the level at which
Muhammad's mortal remains lie within the tombs.

Every mosque contains a kiblah, *indicating the direction of the Kaaba in Mecca. This one, which is inset with highly polished marble tiles and framed by a scalloped brass staircase, was once used by the Prophet Muhammad himself for his daily obsequies.*

53

From their colder climate, Europeans were later to accuse Muhammad of sensuality. The historian Edward Gibbon, in many ways an admirer of Muhammad, went so far as to suggest, in a Latin footnote, that the Prophet could satisfy eleven women in the course of an hour. Significantly, such accusations would only have impressed Arabians, who admire sexual prowess. Nor did the charge offend the spirit of Islam, whose sexual laws were designed to prevent social conflict, not subdue the flesh in the ascetic's sense. In any case the charge hardly bears a moment's scrutiny. Muhammad was certainly susceptible to female charms; he is said to have listed the love of women with prayer and perfume as the things he most enjoyed. But a man who, in his vigorous youth, had stuck to a woman fifteen years his senior was hardly one ruled by the flesh, even if his new responsibilities had left time for prodigious indulgence, which they did not. Several of his new marriages were with women who had lost husbands fighting for Islam; others strengthened his links with important men or powerful tribes.

What captured the lasting allegiance of his people, then, was the message Muhammad brought, not his role as messenger, with its diplomatic skills and marital alliances. Here his achievement both parallels and contrasts with Christianity's. The church, like Islam, had satisfied the metaphysical hunger of a disjointed world. In the Christian case, the world was that of Mediterranean paganism and the disjointedness came from the obliteration of old loyalties in the vast new Roman empire. In the case of Islam, the hunger came from the emptiness of Arabian paganism and the disjointedness resulted from rapid urbanization, which transformed Mecca into a financial metropolis. But acceptance of Christianity in, say, Egypt had meant the total repudiation by a people of their historical legacy. The descendants of Pharaoh's soldiers had come to identify with Pharaoh's enemies, the nomadic Jews—and in the process the Copts (Egyptian Christians) had busily destroyed whatever they could of their cultural heritage, abandoning hieroglyphics, smashing statues, and defacing temples. Muhammad recognized that the free Bedouin of Arabia could hardly contemplate such an alienation from their ancient culture. And so he contrived to synthesize—in part by distorting—the pagan traditions of his people with the mythology of the Semitic prophets as laid out in the Old Testament.

This process of synthesis resembles what grammarians call crasis, the blending or mixture of constituents. Crasis characterizes most religions. The Christian church, for example, was to adopt December 25, the birthday of the sun god, for Jesus—and many a cathedral rose on the site of a pagan temple. Usually, such crasis is effected by later generations; in the case of Islam, by contrast, it was effected in the Prophet's lifetime and under his guidance.

And it began almost immediately after his arrival in Medina. In Mecca, for instance, Muhammad's revelations had made frequent reference to Moses; in Medina, where he learned much from the Jews who refused to join him, Muhammad concentrated on Abraham, or Ibrahim, the patriarch whom the Old Testament named as the ancestor of Arab and Jew alike. Ibrahim's quest for the One God antedated the delivery of the Torah to Moses and of the Gospel, which Muhammad seems to have pictured as a book, to Jesus. The saga of Ibrahim

Not until 630, the eighth year of the Hejira, was Muhammad able to return in triumph to Mecca, his dream of an Arabia united under Islam realized at last. The Prophet's first act was to proclaim a general amnesty, sparing the holy city bloodshed of the sort Medina had witnessed. His second act was to purge the Kaaba of its pagan idols, symbols of pre-Islamic Arabia's divided religious fealties. Henceforth the peoples of the Island of the Arabs would pray to a single god, Allah, to whom Muhammad rededicated both the Kaaba and its foremost pagan totem, the Black Stone (left). This task finished, the Prophet repaired almost immediately to Medina, and soon thereafter he died. From this point his ministry was carried forward by disciples such as Ali, seen at right preaching at the Sacred Mosque.

was used to underpin new rites for Mecca in general and the Kaaba in particular.

It is uncertain what linkage, if any, had existed in the Age of Ignorance between the Arabians' Kaaba, or Ancient House, and the Old Testament. Jewish visitors to Mecca, at a time when ingress was unrestricted, may have thought that their forefather Abraham had been connected with the ancient building. If so, they had hazy notions of geography, for the Bible sets Abraham's career much further north, in the fertile crescent linking the southern borders of Anatolia with the land of Canaan. Be this as it may, the Koran boldly connects Mecca with events in the life of Ibrahim, the first monotheist and "friend of God." The sacred course traditionally run between Shafa and Marwa commemorates the biblical Hagar's desperate search in the wilderness for water for herself and Ismail, her son by Ibrahim. Zemzem, which Muhammad's grandfather had cleared out and walled with masonry, became identified with the well opened by Gabriel to save mother and child. Ismail, as a youth, had helped his father rebuild the Kaaba. An animal substitute saved Ismail, not Isaac as in the Hebrew version, from his father's knife:

For this was an evident trial:
And with a splendid sacrifice we ransomed him.

These new biblical terms of reference for his birthplace were as important for Muhammad as the military levies that were to effect its Islamization. Thanks to the new ideology behind the new terms and the new levies, the transformation of Mecca was no mere change of fashion. It was to last.

The conquest of Mecca took place toward the end of Year Eight, or in January 630. Morale in Mecca had collapsed since the signing of the treaty. The older oligarchs remained unreconciled in their hearts, but the new generation was increasingly won for the Prophet. In his triumphant advance south Muhammad now commanded an army of four columns. (One was led by Khalid ibn Walid, who had led the reprisal raid against Medina in Year Three.) Muhammad facilitated his victory by announcing a general amnesty. The few exceptions included those who had persisted in anti-Islamic propaganda and those guilty of particular violence.

The city fell without serious resistance, and the two or three weeks Muhammad spent in his birthplace were

*Muslim hagiographers drew upon allusions in the
Koran to conjure up tales as marvelous as they were
mythical. In these pictures the artist imagines the glory
of a welcome in the heavens.*

occupied in cleaning the Kaaba. The Ancient House,
rebuilt in Muhammad's youth, contained a number of
paintings as well as idols and fetishes. According to the
historian Azraqi, Muhammad himself stood in front of
the representation of Mary holding Jesus on her lap
and prevented its destruction. (It was to perish a generation later in a fire.) This story is significant for two
reasons. It underlines the respect Muhammad felt for
Jesus and his mother, and it indicates that Muhammad
felt no particular prejudice against representational art.
"Even at the present day," Professor K. A. C. Creswell
has written, "the belief is very widely held that all forms
of painting are forbidden by explicit passages in the
Qurān, but this is a popular error, for no such passages
exist, as Orientalists have frequently pointed out."
Creswell himself dated the change in attitude toward
representational art as coming near the end of the
eighth century and attributed it to three factors: "the
inherent temperamental dislike of Semitic races for human representations in sculpture and painting"; the influence of distinguished Jewish converts to Islam; and
"the feeling, so common among primitive peoples, that
the maker of an image or painting in some way trans-
fers part of the personality of the subject to the image
or painting, and in so doing acquires magical powers
over the person reproduced."

In sum, Muhammad destroyed the pagan idols in the
Kaaba, and at his orders his followers destroyed similar
idols in other Hijazi shrines, because they were symbols
of beings whom their cultists falsely regarded as sharers
in the power of God. This did not apply to representations of Jesus, an envoy of God whom Muhammad believed to have predicted his own career.

IV

Hajj to the Ancient House

On June 8, 632, Muhammad died at Medina in the arms of Ayesha. Some later legends were to ascribe Muhammad's death to the delayed effects of poison. In truth, the Prophet had labored under great strain since his first revelation and, especially after he had become ruler as well as Prophet, he had made many difficult decisions. These, coupled with the ardors of campaigning on a man no longer young, had reduced Muhammad's physical resistance. And fever was endemic in the flat lands around Medina, with its pools of standing water.

Muhammad seems not to have foreseen how near he was to the end of his mission, for he was busy planning a reprisal raid north into Transjordan at the time of his final illness. He was confined to bed for some days and his followers, heartened when he appeared to rally, were stunned when they heard the sound of wailing from the women's quarters. So compelling was the impact of Muhammad's personality—even upon men with secular talents greater than his own—that the news of his death was heard with disbelief. His shouting followers milled outside the small opening that led from the public courtyard of the Prophet's palace to Ayesha's hut. Could God's Messenger die? And if he could, who would replace him as Islam's leader?

It was Muhammad's father-in-law and closest friend, Abu Bakr, who answered the first question. He silenced the incredulous by reciting a verse from the Prophet's as yet unpublished revelations. Only now was its full import clear:

> Muhammad is only a messenger: many are the
> messengers who have died before him: if he dies,
> or is slain, will you turn back on your heels?

The same day, in an instance of democratic election almost unique in Islamic history, the question of leadership was resolved in favor of Abu Bakr. Three years younger than his departed friend, he became Muhammad's first successor (or Caliph, from the Arabic *khalifah*). Abu Bakr was not recognized as a prophet, a role that ended with Muhammad, but as head of the Islamic nation, or *ummah*.

With the two questions answered, Muhammad's body, which had been left unattended for a day in the confusion attending his passing, was washed, shrouded, and interred under the floor of Ayesha's house. Over this simple grave was to rise a mosque regarded as almost as holy as the Kaaba, a mosque in which one prayer is worth a thousand prayers anywhere else. In time it was to hold the tombs of Abu Bakr and Omar as well. Muhammad himself had once said, "The best grave is one you can wipe away with your hand"—meaning a simple pit in the desert sand.

Muhammad's last major act had been to make the full pilgrimage to Mecca, which he undertook in the March before he died. Because of its timing it is known to Muslims as the Pilgrimage of Farewell. Apart from the Koran, which a quarter of humanity attributes to God's direct inspiration, the transformation of the pagan *hajj* represents what is arguably Muhammad's most important contribution to Islam. Obligatory, spectacular, and unifying, this rite maintained a vital, sustaining link among the followers of Muhammad, who were to spread his message thousands of miles, reaching Spain in the west and the limits of China in the east.

For good or bad, the *hajj* preserved forever the bond between all forms of Islam, however geographically re-

mote, and their place of origin, the barren Hijaz. Whether we study this peculiar institution as historians, and attribute its development to a man's careful planning, or as Muslims, and believe that each step was prompted by God, we are equally impressed. The twentieth-century novelist E. M. Forster has suggested that genius lies in the ability to connect. By that definition Muhammad's connection of the pagan ceremonies he had known as a boy with the ideological superstructure revealed in the Koran was indeed a work of rare genius and inspiration. And the *hajj* itself is clearly a project to which Muhammad devoted careful thought, as both the text of the scriptures and the testament of contemporary Muslim chroniclers confirm. Whereas the holy book leaves vague the important question of the hours of prayer, the revelations are specific about the obligation of the pilgrimage, its cardinal actions, and its spirit. "No obscenity," the Koran insists, "nor wickedness, nor wrangling in the *hajj.*" The sacrifice of animals is called for, but the scriptures caution the faithful that "it is not their meat nor their blood that reaches God: it is your piety that reaches him."

If Muhammad did consult others, he sought counsel only from his closest intimates—and he may well have pondered alone, for his deliberation seems to have puzzled his followers. After the purification of the Kaaba in Year Eight, for example, they had expected him to return at the head of the pilgrims in Year Nine. Instead, he stayed in Medina, busying himself with tribal matters. Embassy after camel-back embassy arrived in Mecca to submit to the new Islamic state, but instead of journeying to Mecca himself the Prophet sent a contingent of pilgrims under the leadership of Abu Bakr, who

was apparently joined by Ali en route. Once in Mecca, either Abu Bakr or Ali—traditions dispute as to which—delivered a solemn ultimatum to those who still ascribed partners to God: after a four-month period of grace, they must either make the Islamic confession of faith—"No god but God and Muhammad is the Messenger of God!"—or accept war to the death. Thus, by Year Ten, the holy city had been purified—first of the idols, then of the idolaters—and Muhammad could perform the pilgrimage. In March 632 he set out on the journey south, aware that his last action would be studied, remembered, and made the basis of tradition.

In this he was absolutely correct: the *hajj* as he perfected it became one of the five pillars of Islam (the others being confession of faith, prayer, alms-giving, and daylight fasting in Ramadan). For the city of Mecca itself the *hajj* constituted a unique legacy, one that compensated in part for the political prestige and economic hegemony it had lost and would not recover. Although a verse of the Koran stipulated that pilgrims could combine business dealings with their religious duties, the periodic trading brought to Mecca by the *hajj* proved no substitute for the city's former financial primacy. A provincial city ruled by governors appointed from such caliphal capitals as Damascus or Baghdad—or, later, by semi-autonomous sharifs claiming Korayshi descent—Mecca could not even rival such capitals as Cordoba in southern Spain or Cairo in Egypt, where rival dynasts established anti-caliphates that were to endure for centuries. Mecca's compensation was something less transitory: in Islam, which was also a state and a culture, it was to hold a permanent place at the very heart of the religion founded by Muhammad.

What was once a trickle has become a torrent: more than two million pilgrims now make the annual hajj *to Mecca, turning what was once the most purely Arabian of cities into the most polyglot metropolis in the world. The journey, which used to take months or even years to complete, can be made today by chartered jetliner, the mode of travel by which the chador-clad pilgrims below have come to Mecca. Others—the group of Malaysians at near left, for example—arrive by sea. Where creaking dhows once tied up alongside the wharfs of Jiddah, huge liners now negotiate for berthage, their decks jammed with* hajjis *in* ihram, *the traditional white garb of the pilgrim. Once ashore, the faithful clamber aboard one of the ancient buses (right) that will transport them inland to Mecca.*

61

To almost all Westerners, Islam and Arabia are synonymous—when, in truth, the majority of Muhammad's followers are ebony-skinned natives of such Central African states as Niger and Chad, Cameroun and Gabon, or amber-skinned inhabitants of distant Bangladesh and Burma. Cock a sharp ear in the streets of Mecca during the season of the hajj *and you will hear every tongue humans speak, with the possible exceptions of Eskimo and Finnish—a measure both of the ubiquity of Islam and the spiritual traction that Mecca exerts on the faithful. Keep a sharp eye peeled and you will spot faces as fascinating and as varied as those seen on these two pages.*

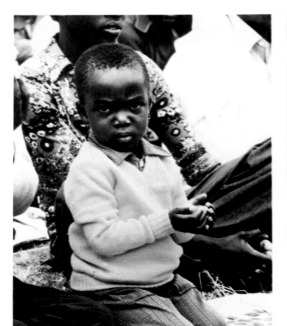

Two religious fiats ennobled the city of Muhammad's birth. The first involved the direction in which the faithful should prostrate themselves in prayer. At a time when Muhammad had hoped that the Jews would endorse his claims, Muslims had prayed toward Jerusalem. An ancient tradition identifies Jerusalem as the point of departure in Muhammad's mystical journey by night to the Seventh Heaven, there to converse with God about prayer: "Praise him, who traveled in one night with his servant from the sacred mosque [in Mecca] to the farthest mosque [Masjid al-Aksa, as the mosque near Jerusalem's Dome of the Rock is known]." The Kaaba has remained the *kiblah* to the present day. Every mosque, including Muhammad's mosque at Medina, has a niche, or *mihrab*, indicating the direction of Mecca. Since the Kaaba stands at its center, the Sacred Mosque at Mecca is the one place on earth where a worshiper can validly pray from every compass point.

It is the second fiat, however, that was to prove the more important, for it emphasized Mecca's link with Ibrahim and his primal act of obedience: "Pilgrimage thereto is a duty men owe to God—those who can afford the journey." By these two basic requirements—prostration and pilgrimage—and by the intuitive skill with which they were knit together, Mecca extended its magnetic centrality beyond the limits of Arabia to command, in our century, souls from all over the world. Mecca became the one spot on the planet that each Muslim, whatever his nationality, aspired to visit at least once before his death, there to perform the rituals fixed by the Prophet.

Muhammad, like other pilgrims, assumed the state known as *ihram* as he approached the sacred territory—and well before he reached its boundary. At the time *ihram* basically signified the sacred state in which the pilgrim put himself at the start of the pilgrimage; it also meant the garb that symbolized this condition. In pagan times the Koraysh had been allowed to perform the rites of pilgrimage in normal attire; others had to perform them in total nudity or obtain, for a price, special clothing from the Koraysh. Muhammad standardized pilgrims' garb by donning two lengths of white and seamless cloth. One length was wrapped round his body from midriff to the knees. The other was thrown around the torso so that it partly covered the left shoulder, the back, and the chest; it was then knotted on the right shoulder.

Women who made the *hajj* were permitted to wear ordinary clothes, provided they covered all parts of their bodies except face and hands. Muhammad, having established a dress code for both males and females, also codified the places at which the pilgrim put on his *ihram*. In the case of those, like the Prophet, who came south on the Medina road, it was a place named Dhu al-Hulufa. Once arrayed in the white clothing, which was donned after ablutions and a final haircut, Muhammad decreed, the pilgrim must not cut his hair or nails, indulge in sexual intercourse, shed blood, hunt animals, uproot plants, wear shoes (although a kind of sandal was permissible), or cover his head (although he might use a sunshade). In one respect, and one respect only, Muhammad lightened the previous bans—by abolishing the Korayshite stipulation that only Meccan food could be consumed on the pilgrimage.

Once attired, the Prophet, like millions after him, set his face toward Mecca, still some distance to the south.

From the first the availability of accommodations in Mecca has lagged behind the pilgrims' needs—and with the exponential growth of religious tourism in the past few decades this shortfall has become chronic. Hundreds of thousands of hajjis simply camp out in the city's narrow streets, making the threat of epidemic a very present fear and turning all Mecca into one vast souk. Barbers set up shop among the soup kettles, shearing the faithful in preparation for their pilgrimage. And exhausted hajjis catnap wherever space permits, ignoring as best they can the clangor of the crowds and the searing rays of the Arabian sun.

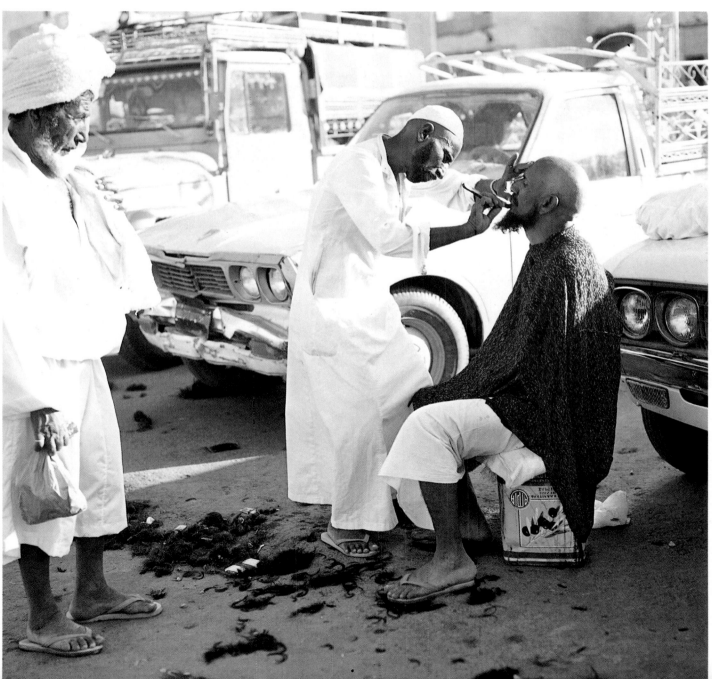

A caprice of nature has given the Island of the Arabs a superabundance of oil and a dismaying dearth of drinkable water—and both these factors have been of inestimable consequence in shaping the peninsula's history. It was the existence of potable water that permitted the establishment of a permanent settlement at Mecca, and when events transformed the settlement into a religious center, they also transmogrified the well known as Zemzem (left) into a holy font. Since time immemorial the Arabs have marked the passage of the hours by sundials like the one seen at right but used a lunar calendar to record the passing of years. Which is why the hajj *falls sometimes in cool November—and sometimes in the insufferable heat of July.*

From this moment on, one prayer was chanted repeatedly. Its Arabic refrain, *labbaika allahumma labbaika,* can be roughly translated as "I am here, God, at your command!" Some scholars believe that in ancient days Iblis, or the devil, was included in this salutation, in much the same way that the ancient Egyptians had both despised and worshiped Set, the god of disorder. No such practice was permitted in Islam.

Muhammad's first major innovation was his decision to include in the *hajj*—which was to take place solely between the ninth and twelfth days of Dhul-Hijja, the twelfth lunar month—the *'umrah,* known to Europeans as the lesser pilgrimage. The *'umrah* pilgrim kissed the Black Stone and then performed seven circumambulations of the Kaaba. These began at the Black Stone and were conducted in a counterclockwise direction. The first three circuits were made at a brisk pace, the last four more slowly. The Black Stone was then kissed again, water from Zemzem was drunk, and the pilgrim proceeded to make the ritual course between Shafa and Marwa. Muhammad performed his course on camelback, covering the distance seven times and ending at Marwa. The course constituted a gentle run of just over four hundred yards.

In pagan times the *'umrah* had evidently been a local, Meccan festival, one that does not seem to have attracted pilgrims from further afield. We have no independent evidence as to the complete pagan rite, although it was almost certainly richer and wilder than the bare essentials that survive. The *'umrah* was originally linked with Rajab, the seventh lunar month, at a time when that month was as firmly locked to the spring as the three *hajj* months were to the autumn. This was

achieved through the Meccan practice, already noted, of periodically inserting extra days into the lunar calendar to bring it into phase with the solar year. In his pilgrimage sermon, Muhammad explicitly condemned intercalation, as this practice is technically known; those who transposed a month, the argument went, muddled up what God had made sacred with what God had intended to be secular.

That the *'umrah* survives at all is probably due to the Prophet's decision to incorporate its essential rites—the circling of the Kaaba after kissing the Black Stone, and then the running of the sacred course—into his farewell *hajj.* Although the Meccan fiesta was to become less festive, losing its seasonal link with the spring, it still involved merriment and pageant when Ibn Jubayr, a pilgrim from Muslim Spain, visited the holy city in 1183. Still associated with Rajab, the *'umrah* that Ibn Jubayr described took place in autumn, between October 20 and November 18, thanks to the "purified" lunar calendar. "That night," Ibn Jubayr recalled, "the Sacred Mosque was filled with brightly shining lamps." He continued:

When the seeing of the new moon had been proven before the Emir, he ordered the beating of tymbals and drums and the sounding of trumpets as a sign that it was the night of the festival. When the morning of that night of Thursday came, he set forth on the *'umrah* with a vast concourse the like of which has never been heard of. The people of Mecca collected round him to the last person, and went forth according to their ranks, tribe by tribe, quarter by quarter, bristling with weapons, on horse and on foot, assembling in numbers too numer-

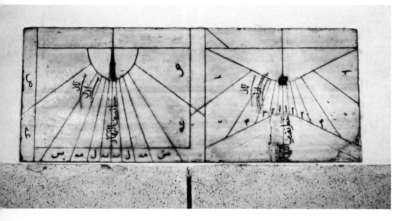

OVERLEAF: It is said that the Kaaba is never left untended, that even when mortals are absent the sacred site is constantly circled by some 70,000 angels. (The occasional rippling of the kiswa, *the heavy drapery covering the Kaaba, is traditionally laid not to the wind but to this celestial host.) The question is academic, however, for the press of pilgrims around the ancient structure—which they call Baytallah, God's House—is so great that few* hajjis *ever get close enough to kiss the Black Stone or touch the* kiswa *itself. Even at night, when this extraordinary time-lapse photograph was taken, the sacred precinct is thronged with pilgrims, circumambulating the Kaaba in accordance with rituals established by the Prophet.*

ous to count. . . . They set forth in admirable order; the cavaliers left on their horses and playing with their weapons, while the foot leaped upon each other vying in skill-at-arms. They carried spears, swords and targe, and appeared to pierce with the spear, strike with the sword, and defend with the targe with which they protected themselves, revealing all manner of marvels in their skilful contests. They hurled their spears into the air, and hastened after them to catch them in their hands, although at times the course of the weapons brought them on to their heads, they being in such a press that they had no chance to manoeuvre.

The emir next presided in an open space at a species of tournament, after which he circumambulated the Kaaba, led by reciters of the Koran, while from the roof of the dome over the Zemzem fountain its particular muezzin raised his voice in good wishes, compliments, and prayers. The emir prayed at the Kaaba's southeast wall and then paid his devotions to the Station of Ibrahim. (This was a boulder, apparently kept inside the Kaaba at that time and brought outside for special devotions. It was placed under a wooden dome and after prayers the dome was lifted so that the emir could kiss the boulder.) The ruler then left the mosque by the Bab al-Safa for the place of ritual running, where he performed the sacred course on horseback, preceded by spearmen and hemmed in by his officers. After he retired to his dwelling the place of running surged with men and women performing the ritual course between the hillocks. By this time these hills had almost certainly become engulfed by urban building as Mecca, like other much-built-on sites, rose on its detritus.

Muhammad's inclusion of what had been a Meccan spring feast in the originally autumnal *hajj* produced what a non-Muslim authority on the subject has called "the banal *'umrah* of Islamic orthodoxy." Certainly the factors that made the lesser pilgrimage picturesque, even as late as the twelfth century, have weakened steadily. Nowadays it can be performed at any time of the year. The pilgrim wears *ihram,* kisses the Black Stone, circumambulates the Kaaba (or, if arthritic, may even be pushed around it in a wheelbarrow), and performs the ritual course—but in so doing does not fulfill his obligation to make the *hajj,* for the *'umrah* now has the character of a supererogatory work, an action additional to those required by religious law.

One reason for the *'umrah's* relative decline may be that certain aspects, indelibly pagan, seem to have worried devout Muslims from a relatively early time. One tradition has Omar, the second Caliph, addressing the Black Stone in the following terms:

> I know well that you are a stone which can do neither good nor evil, and unless I had seen the Prophet, on whom be prayer and the blessings of God, kiss you, I would not kiss you.

When attributed to Omar, who was, like Muhammad, brought up to the ancient devotions, this objection sounds less than plausible. It more probably reflects the scruples of Sufyan, the terminal source for this particular chain of tradition. Sufyan is known to have been a Sufi, or mystic, and as such he may have jibbed at the excessive devotion traditional Muslims gave to the Kaaba and to anthropomorphic survivals in the popular

cult of the Black Stone. One persistent legend, for example, identified the stone with the angel that had guarded Adam in Paradise, saying that when Adam was exiled to earth the angel became a stone. Endowed with a tongue, it will on the Day of Judgment speak up for those of the faithful who have paid it honor.

One detail of Muhammad's *hajj* that was not generally repeated was his rest between the completion of the *'umrah* and the start of the main pilgrimage. Interrupting his state of *ihram,* he was entitled to enjoy normal relations with his wives—although weariness, not uxoriousness, is the most likely explanation for his pause. And while he rested Muhammad received a revelation defining the sacrifice a man must make for allowing himself this indulgence. In later times, those making the pilgrimage ran *'umrah* and *hajj* together and the state of *ihram* was not discontinued until the completion of both.

The focus of the *hajj* proper is not the Kaaba but a conical granite hill some miles east of Mecca and outside the sacred territory (see diagram, page 166). It rises almost two hundred feet above a desert plain on the main road to Ta'if. The name of the hill—'Arafat—is of uncertain derivation, although pious legend claims that Adam and Eve met here after their expulsion from Eden, and greeted each other with a cry of recognition—connected, in Arabic, with the verb *'arafa.* The hill is known popularly as the Mount of Mercy, or Jabal al-Rahma: the last noun closely corresponding to the first of the two epithets, the Merciful, the Compassionate, repeatedly applied by Muslims to God. The crux of the *hajj* is the "standing," or mass assembly, on the slopes of Mount Arafat on the ninth day of Dhul-Hijja.

This standing begins immediately after the sun reaches its zenith and lasts until sunset. The pilgrims mass on the flanks of the bare hill or in the plain below. Like the kissing of the Black Stone, the circumambulation of the Kaaba, and the ritual course, this assembly finds parallels elsewhere in Middle Eastern religion. The Book of Exodus uses the Hebrew equivalent for *hajj* in a passage where God commands the Israelites to perform a feast for him, one at which all the males must appear before the Lord. As mentioned earlier, some scholars take the parallel further and link the *hajj*, originally an autumn feast, with the Jewish autumnal Feast of Booths, or Succoth.

In his sermon from Mount Arafat, Muhammad introduced other changes besides the abolition of intercalation, which severed any connection between the *hajj* and a particular season. One change was not entirely successful. In earlier times, the moment the sun set pilgrims had rushed west to the nearby plain of Muzdalifa, roughly halfway from Arafat to Mina, the place where Ibrahim was believed to have offered Ismail in sacrifice. Muhammad counseled a more sedate pace, but some archetypal impulse kept this a chaotic occasion, and parties of pilgrims have often been parted from one another and sometimes even trampled on. The pilgrims spent the night at Muzdalifa, and at sunrise they rushed on to Mina to sacrifice animals and pelt three standing stones. (Muhammad changed the time of departure from sunrise to pre-dawn, probably to remove one further link with a solar cult.) The pagan significance of pelting standing stones has been variously interpreted, some even seeing it as a form of honor to the gods. More probably, in the context of Muzdalifa, with its tutelary thunder god and its fierce Meccan climate, the stoning of primitive sun symbols, or obelisks, represented an assault on the tyrannical sun, for autumn's thunderstorms heralded cooler weather and the sudden greening of the desert. Muhammad identified the obelisks with "Satan the Stoned." Once the animals had been slain and eaten, either by the pilgrims who dedicated them or by the watching poor—and once the symbols of evil had been struck by the right number of pebbles of the right size—the *hajj* ended with a farewell visit to Mecca. Once again the Black Stone was kissed, the Ancient House circumambulated, and Zemzem water drunk. The barbered pilgrim was then free to depart.

Muhammad's liturgical genius is proved by the durability of the *hajj* as he perfected it. The purist may identify and criticize its pagan elements, yet it was in retaining these very elements that the Prophet showed his intuitive understanding of the religious spirit and of the role symbolic actions can play as a religion's fixed stars. But deeper than the significance of any one symbolic survival—the circumambulation, for instance, which had been a cult feature in other Semitic shrines—was the spirit of magical exactitude in which the *hajj* was thenceforth conducted. For despite the insistence of many theologians that intention is all-important, on the popular level the *hajj* is a magical rite backed by deep, unconscious forces. The essence of its magic lies in precise adherence to a hieratic phrase or action. And just as a spell becomes invalid if one syllable is mispronounced, so the *hajj* becomes invalid if a prayer is made in the wrong place or by the wrong formula. The right number of stones of the right size must be cast at the devils the right number of times; they must hit their mark and they must not have been thrown already by another pilgrim.

The need to get such things totally right may induce anxiety, and, as we shall see, it produces the need for a caste of professional guides. But, conversely, when the rites are properly performed, all anxiety and self-doubt dissolve in the satisfaction of ceremonies that conform to a long-established tradition. The Muslim pilgrim has the sensation of standing, at some expense, with countless generations of forebears and forerunners. *"Labbaika allahumma labbaika*—I am here, God, at your command."* And here, too, stand those of his ancestors who were able to make the pilgrimage in earlier times. And before them the legendary shades of the Companions of the Prophet, of the Prophet's wives, of the illustrious Caliphs, poets, and thinkers of Islam. And even before them, to the believer in the Koran, a chain of prophets and pious Arabians stretches back to Ibrahim and even Adam. And, for those whose imagination can travel to the God-lit world before the creation of this planet, to the Paradise from which Adam descended to remodel the Kaaba upon terra firma.

Such ceremonies give a sense of continuity and serenity to the pilgrim. On a different level, an American convert of the 1970s suggests another aspect: "The sheer organized mindlessness of people doing the same thing is therapeutic."

V

Changes and Constants

Mecca, which soared to its zenith immediately before and during Muhammad's lifetime, was afterwards a spent rocket. This exhaustion was not apparent to the Prophet's immediate successors, however, who saw the first stage of Mecca's decline as nothing more than a welcome relaxation of past tensions. In Islam's first century Mecca and Medina became, for a time, cities of hedonistic retreat. While Muslim armies fought their way across North Africa and beyond the Persian plateau, some of the booty acquired through this empire-building was spent on palaces in the two cities. The Arabian version of the good life, with its music and musicians, dancing girls and heady perfumes, was lived in an enriched Mecca that even boasted a club where such games as backgammon and chess could be played. The vaguely precious literature of the period emphasized ephemeral love.

But in life, unlike literature, function is often fate— and the removal of political decision from Arabia left its proudest city, Mecca, with no option but to eke out a living from a service industry akin to tourism. Pilgrim shrines, like beauty spots, diminish those who profit from them. In ceasing to be a place of mercantile venture, in staking its future fortune on the influx of pilgrims, Mecca nurtured a populace that showed no further signs of miraculous potential. How great this potential had been, albeit briefly, appears from even the most cursory glance at the men of the Prophet's generation.

Orthodox Muslims have accorded unique respect to Muhammad's first four successors, "the Rightly Guided Caliphs," and with good reason. When the great Byzantine cathedral of Hagia Sophia was finally captured by the Ottoman sultan Muhammad II, its rich mosaics were covered with white plaster and the church became Constantinople's most impressive mosque. The chief decorations were huge plaques bearing the monograms of Abu Bakr, Omar, Uthman, and Ali. Nine centuries after their deaths, these four Meccans and their spiritual leader had come to dominate the former "New Rome" of Emperor Constantine. All had been Companions of the Prophet (the phrase later acquired an almost technical meaning), and all were related to him by marriage. Daughters of Abu Bakr and Omar had been married to Muhammad; Muhammad had given daughters in marriage to Uthman and to his cousin Ali. Each of the four contributed significantly to Islam and, except for Abu Bakr, each died by the assassin's knife.

Abu Bakr, a lean warrior whose sole vanity was his hennaed beard, outlived Muhammad by only two years. Yet his brief period of power coincided with a life-and-death challenge to the new religion. It was he who had asked the Koranic question—"If he dies, or is slain, will you turn back on your heels?"—and he who discovered that many Arabian tribes were in fact turning away from Islam. In view of Bedouin tradition, this was hardly surprising. The tribes that had accepted Muhammad as ruler saw their bond in terms of fealty to an exceptional individual—a supersheikh who promised both material and spiritual rewards. With his death in A.D. 632, the bond snapped. Abu Bakr's prompt military and diplomatic action won over the rebellious tribesmen, restoring Arab unity and making possible the great missionary wars that later spread the faith of Muhammad. Islam owed its survival as a political force to the single-minded energy of Abu Bakr.

On his death Abu Bakr left to his successor, Omar, a reunited Arabia to use as a fortress and as a reserve of soldiers. Omar ruled for ten years before being murdered by a Christian slave of the Muslim governor of Basra. (The slave's motive, although unrecorded, was probably resentment at the heavy taxes levied by this ruler, who was as severe on members of his household as he was on his subjects.) Omar masterminded campaigns that laid the foundation of a world-state and set an example, too little followed, of inflexible integrity.

The third Caliph, Uthman, lacked both Abu Bakr's burning faith and Omar's organizing genius. His outstanding characteristic, according to tradition, was the attention he paid to his personal appearance. He promoted the interests of the aristocratic Omayyad family, to which he belonged, in ill-omened anticipation of the nepotism that was to weaken later dynasties. Yet this somewhat rarified patrician nonetheless did Islam the inestimable service of establishing the text of its holy book. By presenting copies of the Koran, in a text approved by himself, to Damascus, Basra, and Kufa, as well as Medina and Mecca, and by ordering that all variants should be destroyed, he liberated Muslims then and now from the sort of textual confusion that had plagued earlier faiths. After a reign of fourteen years, during which Islam's primitive unity showed increasing signs of schism, Uthman was slain while reading his Koran: intruders burst into his house and spilled his blood over the very text he had secured.

Uthman's murder started a cycle of overt violence that Ali, the fourth Caliph, was unable to halt. The closest by kinship to Muhammad of all four Caliphs, Ali is generally accounted the first male Muslim; he was certainly the ancestor of all the Prophet's descendants. He possessed the qualities of an Islamic saint: generous, eloquent, and brave, he also had an otherworldly attitude toward human life. "The world is carrion," he said, "and whoever wants part of it must be satisfied to live with dogs." The compromises necessary in the political life that had been thrust upon him were beyond Ali's mastering and he was assassinated in A.D. 661 in the mosque at Kufa, his Iraqi capital. The fact that he was brought down by the more ruthless Omayyads—who blamed Ali's followers for Uthman's murder and who founded a successor caliphate based in Damascus—has endeared Ali to groups that have opposed or despised the Islamic establishment. The poor and the oppressed, the enslaved and the radical, have often chosen to belong to the party of Shia, of Ali, or have felt an affinity to it.

These first Caliphs were only four among a host of remarkable Meccans who were contemporaries of Muhammad. Khalid ibn Walid's strategic flair and spectacular conquests would win him a place in any manual of war; his rival, the astute Amr ibn al-As, not only conquered Egypt but, unlike Khalid, whose fate it was to tangle with Omar and suffer demotion at the height of his career, survived into old age. These outstanding men—and many, many others hallowed in Arab memory—belonged to an emigrant generation. They moved, not simply from Mecca to Medina, but outwards from Arabia into surrounding countries. Whole tribes of warriors, motivated by the pioneers' dedication to both idealism and greed, left the Island of the Arabs, most never to return. Thousands died in battle. Many thousands more resettled in military cantons designed, like

One of the earliest extant eyewitness accounts of Mecca was written by ibn Jubayr, who made the hajj in the 1180s from Moorish Spain. This pilgrimage, which took two years to complete, was neither overlong nor particularly arduous by contemporary standards. Significantly, ibn Jubayr could have made his long journey without ever leaving Muhammad's spiritual empire, for by the twelfth century Islam had spread across all of North Africa, and, borne by the Moors who conquered Spain in 714, it had become firmly entrenched in Iberia. There, in 960, the Caliph al-Hakam II was to erect the great mosque of Cordoba (right), a building whose architectural splendors are celebrated as the apotheosis of Islamic art.

Basra and Kufa, to control the conquered provinces.

At this distance in time, statistics are naturally hard to verify, but it seems almost certain that some degree of overpopulation preceded and powered the great outburst of Islam. What is definite is that Islam's triumphs left Arabia itself with a much diminished population. This was true of every major population center on the peninsula—except Mecca. Like other cities, she exported her male elite as warriors or satraps; but, unlike them, her numbers were replenished. As widening circles of mankind accepted the obligations of Islam, non-Arabian pilgrims visited Mecca in growing multitudes. And the foreigners who settled in the city introduced genetic change. That many settled, rather than return home, was not surprising. Ibn Jubayr's pilgrimage, for instance, took place between 1183 and 1185, at a time when communications from one end of the Mediterranean to the other were comparatively good. Even so, his journey to Mecca, Medina, and the Abbasid caliphal capital of Baghdad kept him away from Spain for a month over two years. (His travels were paid for by the governor of Granada as penance for having forced ibn Jubayr, who served as his secretary, to drink wine in defiance of the Islamic ban.) Poorer pilgrims took far longer, often paying for their travel expenses with bouts of casual labor enroute. And some came from far greater distances than Andalucia.

The results were predictable. Islam had never advocated celibacy for men or women. Except for the few days when the pilgrim entered the state of *ihram*, he was not expected to live like a monk, yet Muslims were often reluctant to take their wives with them on the arduous pilgrimage. There were children at home to be

The cavernous, echoing rotunda of Hagia Sophia, Istanbul's preeminent mosque, provides the attentive visitor with tangible evidence of 1,600 years of religious history. Built by Emperor Constantine as a Christian basilica—a role its huge vaulted architraves and serried lunettes suggest and its magnificent mosaics confirm—Hagia Sophia was captured by the Ottoman sultan Muhammad II in 1453 and promptly converted into a mosque. The former church's offending mosaics were buried beneath layers of plaster and whitewash, and its central chamber (left) was hung with enormous plaques that bear the names of Islam's earliest Caliphs.

cared for, and the roads were notoriously dangerous. A solution that preserved decency, while increasing the non-native population of Mecca, resulted from two concessions to male sexuality revealed to Muhammad. Limited polygamy was permitted by Islamic law, and a marriage could be dissolved by the husband simply saying "I divorce you" three times. (The Shia required two witnesses of this act but the majority of Muslims dispensed with this requirement.) The institution of temporary marriage—with none of the disgrace generally attached to prostitution—thus solved the libidinal problems of many pilgrims. Both parties entered into it open-eyed. The temporary wife was protected by Islamic law, which allowed her to retain her property as well as whatever dowry the marriage contract specified. This system was obviously not ideal, but it did preserve the conscientious pilgrim from a disorderly life, and the children that resulted from such brief liaisons were considered legitimate. Some pilgrims left these children with their mothers after divorcing them and returning home. Others, seduced by the prospect of ending their days in the holy city or genuinely attached to the women they had married, stayed on in Mecca. In any case, the original Arabian stock was, from generation to generation, modified by foreigners. From having been the most typically Arabian city, Mecca became the least—acquiring a cosmopolitanism not of culture but of ethnic background that continues to this day.

It would be delusory to imagine that the pilgrims' sexual appetite was always appeased with such decorum. Piety often acts as a stimulant, the religious emotions being somehow linked with the erotic, and cities particularly devoted to religion have often enjoyed un-

savory reputations. Old Jerusalem's temple prostitutes and sacred sodomites posed problems for at least two Hebrew kings, while vice flourished spectacularly in the sunlight of Rome's papal court. Men on pilgrimage, like men on campaign or holiday, feel freed from everyday restraints and the prying eyes of neighbors. And so, despite official Islamic disapproval, Medina and Mecca were renowned for their whores as early as the Omayyad period (A.D. 661–750). More than a millennium later, a visitor whose morals had been shaped by German protestantism described a situation in which poor prostitutes inhabited a special quarter in north Mecca while "those of the higher order are dispersed over the town. . . .Their outward behaviour is more decent than that of any public women in the East, and it requires the experienced eye of a Makkaway [Meccan] to ascertain by a particular movement in her gait, that the veiled female passing before him belongs to the venal tribe." The same observer complained that the Sacred Mosque itself was "almost publicly and daily contaminated by the practices of the grossest depravity: to these no disgrace is here attached; the young of all classes are encouraged in them by the old, and even parents have been so base as to connive at them for the sake of money. From such pollution, however, the encampments of the Arabian-Bedouin are exempt." According to H. R. P. Dickson, an English authority on the desert, twentieth-century nomads are no better: "Mecca is recognised as one of the most immoral towns in Arabia. If one can believe the Bedawin, every form of foul vice prevails there." A new, puritanical dynasty from the Arabian-Bedouin encampments was prevented from seizing Mecca at the time of the first complaint,

but the same dynasty was to meet the challenge of purifying Mecca in the second half of this century.

Immorality was only part of the problem, however. Assaults on the pilgrims' nostrils, health, and pocket could be more painful than moral affronts. A report compiled in the late 1970s by the Hajj Research Centre at King Abdul Aziz University in Jiddah listed the pilgrims' two main complaints as "the lack of sanitary conditions and the exorbitant prices for everything." Modern quarantine systems and other controls have ensured that Mecca is no longer the source of epidemics that it was in the centuries before Lister and Pasteur. In Mecca's defense it should be noted that even in the early Middle Ages Muslim rulers were already laboring to provide the city with a more palatable water supply than that afforded by the well of Zemzem. A fine canal was built to bring sweet water from springs in the nearby hills, where the stark sun had a sterilizing effect on dirt and the germs it contained. At a time when the average number of pilgrims hovered below a hundred thousand a year, the absence of hygienic niceties can hardly have outraged visitors from a world whose standards were far from those of the twentieth-century suburb.

A Victorian adventurer who managed the pilgrimage in disguise described one horror that cannot have diminished. This resulted from the mass sacrifice at Muna, the climax of the *hajj*. In theory, the pilgrim either consumed his sacrifice himself or distributed it to the poor. But "the days of drying out"—the Arabic phrase for the time when the remains of the carcasses were dried by the sun, often to form rations for the journey home—produced a dreadful stench. "Literally,

the land stank. Five or six thousand animals had been slain and cut up in this Devil's Punchbowl. I leave the reader to imagine the rest. The evil might be avoided by building *abattoirs*, or, more easily still, by digging long trenches, and by ordering all pilgrims, under pain of mulct [fine or penalty], to sacrifice in the same place." By the late 1970s, the slaughtered beasts numbered in excess of a million, and there were few poor people left to eat them. As we shall note in the final chapter, more drastic solutions are being considered.

The exorbitant prices mentioned by the Hajj Research Centre in its report have caused bitter and persistent resentment from earliest times. Pilgrims exhausted by years of travel, tried by bandits, cholera, and tempest, reached the goal of their dreams only to be fleeced by its guardians. Like Lourdes or Capri, all Mecca benefited from the pious influx. But two groups in particular exploited the pilgrims.

First, a clan called the Sons of Shaiba had the right, allegedly granted by the Prophet, to guard the Kaaba, though not the mosque as a whole. The entrance to the Kaaba was through a door set at a man's height above the marbled ground. (It had been raised to this level in A.D. 608 to prevent the periodic floods from invading the interior.) The door was reached in ibn Jubayr's day by a wheeled staircase of nine steps, and the Shaiba kept the key. Not that a visit to the interior of the Kaaba was either obligatory or customary; indeed, there were disadvantages attached to entry. "Those who tread the hallowed floor are bound, among many other things, never again to walk barefooted, to take up fire with the fingers, or to tell lies," reported the Victorian visitor, adding, "mostly really conscientious men can-

"Pilgrimage to the House is a duty unto God for mankind, for he who can find a way thither. As for him who disbelieveth, let him know that lo! God is independent of all creatures," declares the Koran. For those who believe that the Pilgrimage to the House is a duty unto God, the first phase of the hajj—the immutable, centuries-old ceremony through which that duty is discharged—culminates in the tawaf, or ritual circling of the Kaaba. Every pilgrim makes seven counterclockwise circuits of the cube, and every time he passes the southeast corner, where the Black Stone is inset at a height of five feet from the ground, he intones the Koranic line "In the name of God, and God is supreme." The supplicants opposite are seen with their ihram-clad backs forming concentric circles supplicants seen opposite have done, their deeply bowed heads and ihram-clad backs forming concentric circles that radiate out from the base of the Kaaba. For all its spiritual significance, the Kaaba is remarkably free of architectural detail. Its distinctive features are a brass door (above), set high in one of the cube's fifty-foot-high sides, and a filigreed golden drainspout (right) that depends from the roof.

not afford the luxuries of slippers, tongs, and truth." Nor did the Kaaba contain anything of major interest or artistic value. Yet prayers performed inside were believed to confer a blessing, and the Shaiba would open the door for a financial consideration.

The regular days for opening have varied throughout the centuries. In ibn Jubayr's time, for example, the Kaaba was opened on Mondays and Fridays and daily in Rajab. (The twenty-ninth day of Rajab was reserved for women.) Since, as ibn Jubayr explains, many women took their infants and breast-fed babies with them, the following day was devoted to washing the shrine. "When the water poured from the Ka'bah many men and women hastened to it, seeking blessedness by laving their hands and faces in it, and often collecting it in vases they had brought for the occasion." The Shaiba also took charge of the *kiswa*, the annually renewed covering of the Kaaba. Until the twentieth century this covering was traditionally made in Egypt. Its colors changed throughout the centuries, but never its sanctity, and when it had hung for a year against the Ancient House it was felt to be steeped in blessings.

A minority of pilgrims making the *hajj* subsidized the Sons of Shaiba, for no one was obliged by law to buy a piece of the *kiswa*, see the pillars that supported the Kaaba's roof, or study its miscellany of undistinguished treasures. But because of the intricate rites involved in the *hajj*, the need to perform the right movements and to say the right prayers at the right place, the pilgrims were dependent on another, larger caste. Known as *mutawafeen*—those who give instruction in the *tawaf*, or circumambulation—or simply as *deleels*—guides—these provided indispensable services, both in the rituals of the *umrah* and *hajj* and in the day-to-day requirements of living in Mecca. The same Westerner who had condemned the morals of Meccan youth also reported that

the idlest, most impudent, and vilest individuals of Mekka adopt the profession of guides; and as there is no want of those qualities, and a sufficient demand for guides during the Hadj, they are very numerous. Besides the places which I have described in the town, the metowafs accompany the hadjys to all the other places of resort in the sacred district, and are ready to perform every kind of service in the city. But their utility is more than counterbalanced by their importunity and knavery. They besiege the room of the hadjy from sun-rise to sun-set; and will not allow him to do any thing without obtruding their advice: they sit down with him to breakfast, dinner, and supper; lead him into all possible expenses, that they may pocket a share of them; suffer no opportunity to pass of asking him for money; and woe to the poor ignorant Turk who employs them as his interpreter in any mercantile concern.

The guides performed one function not fulfilled by the modern tourist guide: they were prepared temporarily to marry widows, who were otherwise unable to perform the pilgrimage respectably.

Against their critics the guides could argue that the *hajj* season was short and that they needed to lay up enough cash to last them for the rest of the year, when the holy city lapsed once more into its accustomed stagnation. And since the pilgrims conceived of the *hajj* as the spiritual equivalent of the *jihad*—that collective effort the West has translated, not entirely accurately, as "holy war"—they endured the hardships and expenditures as tests accompanying a spiritual odyssey. Until the Industrial Revolution transformed transportation, most pilgrims journeyed on foot. Even Haroun al-Rashid, the most spectacular of Caliphs, made at least one of his nine pilgrimages on foot. (He and his wife Zubaydah made the *hajj* from Baghdad, and every morning a vast carpet was rolled out before them to cover the stretch of desert they would traverse that day.) Ordinary pilgrims sometimes knew safe roads, reliable wells, and adequate supply sources. But when central power weakened under feeble Caliphs or after foreign invasion, pilgrims were obliged to venture through lands where the Bedouin stripped those they did not kill.

Over the centuries the rites of the *hajj* remained essentially the same as those performed by the Prophet, but the buildings and places associated with them were subject to change. The Sacred Mosque, as the world sees it in modern photographs, is totally different from the structure in existence at Muhammad's birth, for instance. This had been a small, unroofed building, more like a sheepfold than a temple. Its retaining walls were at most fifteen feet high and made of rough stone without cement. Within was the well of Zemzem, and without clustered the houses of Mecca's wealthy. By A.D. 608, when a Byzantine ship was fortuitously wrecked on the Red Sea coast, the Kaaba was in a state of delapidation. The ship in question happened to carry a man who was both a carpenter and a mason, and with his help—and the timbers from the wreck—the Koraysh rebuilt the Kaaba. Both his skills were needed, as the new Kaaba was constructed of alternating courses of stone

and wood. A coat of plaster gave it a uniform appearance. The roof was supported by six pillars, and the surfaces of these columns, as well as the walls and ceiling, were ornamented with pictures of trees, angels, and prophets. Because the wrecked ship had been on its way to Abyssinia, it is possible that Baqum, the carpenter-mason, was an Ethiopian and that the Kaaba that Muhammad knew and cleansed was decorated in the style of Abyssinian stone churches.

After Muhammad's death the energetic second Caliph, Omar, bought the houses surrounding the Kaaba and razed them to clear a space for the prostrations of Muslim worship. This space was further enlarged by Uthman ten years later. Abdullah ibn Zubair, a contestant for the caliphate in the second generation after Muhammad's death, rebuilt the Kaaba entirely after it caught fire during a siege of Mecca. He greatly enlarged the structure and replaced the six pillars with three much larger ones. Glass mosaics—once the endowment of a king who invaded Mecca from Yemen in 570, the Year of the Elephant—were employed in its decoration, the first use of such material in an Islamic building. At the time Arabia had no architects of its own, so ibn Zubair imported Persian builders—whose foreign singing was remembered in Mecca long after their work was completed.

Ibn Zubair's Kaaba did not stand for long, however. Twenty years later the ruthless but effective Omayyad governor al-Hajjaj demolished the grandiose structure and remodeled the temple on the lines of the smaller one that had stood in the Prophet's time—establishing the basic shape that has persisted until the present. In the intervening centuries the Kaaba has undergone two

Mecca sits in an arid cup, its rim the bleak and barren hills of the Hijaz. In the season of the hajj, *that cup runneth over: hundreds of thousands of Muslims descend upon the Sacred Mosque, clogging every thoroughfare, alley, and passageway in the city. The* hajjis' *presence, which testifies both to the vitality of Islam and the fervor of its followers, presents an awesome logistical challenge to the Saudi royal house, which assumes primary responsibility for the well-being of the pilgrims during their stay in Mecca. Foremost among the Saudis' obligations is preventing the outbreak of communicable disease, which, in ibn Jubayr's day, posed as much peril for pilgrims as did the Bedouins who preyed upon the caravan routes.*

major assaults. The first came in 930, when a fanatical sect ravaged southern Iraq, the home province of the new Abbasid dynasty based on Baghdad, and then, surging across the desert to the holy city, massacred 50,000 Meccans and carried off the Black Stone to their stronghold by the Persian Gulf. Apparently cracked in three parts in a fire that occurred around 683, the Stone was further chipped during this episode, and when it was returned in 951 its pieces were set in a stone ring held together by a silver band. The second disaster was natural: early in the seventeenth century a major flood engulfed Mecca. The sacred precinct became a lake, and only one wall of the Kaaba was left standing. Rebuilt at that time, it has remained unchanged to the present day.

The Sacred Mosque, which encloses the Kaaba, owes its basic shape—a great oblong surrounded by colonnaded arcades—to the Abbasids. They had plotted and fought their way to dominance through skillful exploitation of Persian resentment over the Arabian chauvinism of the Omayyads. Once in power, the Abbasid Caliph al-Mahdi imported a vast selection of pillars from Egypt to compose his colonnades. His son, Haroun al-Rashid, who figures in so many tales of *The Thousand and One Nights*, contributed a pulpit. But if the structure of the mosque is Abbasid, the general style of the building reflects the four centuries during which the Ottoman Turks maintained their suzerainty over Mecca. Structures built over the Zemzem and the Station of Ibrahim, as well as small edifices used by the four orthodox schools of Islam, all reflected Ottoman taste. Indeed, until the coming of oil wealth in the twentieth century, the style and character of the holy

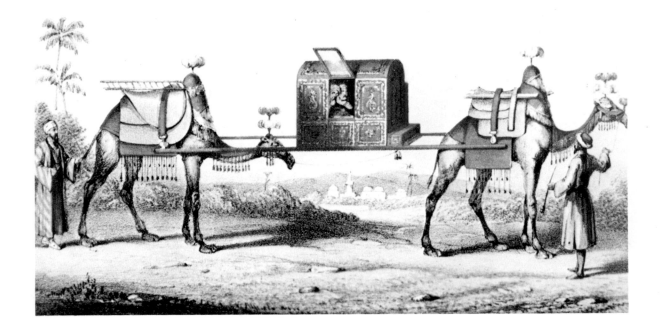

city were meticulously maintained by the descendants of Central Asian nomads.

Since the Prophet's time, control of Medina and Mecca had been essential to any claim to rule Islam. In the interim between the collapse of the Abbasid dynasty in 1258, when the Mongols sacked Baghdad, their capital, and the rise of the Ottoman empire in the early sixteenth century, sovereignty over the Hijaz was claimed and largely exercised by the Mamelukes of Egypt. The Mamelukes, one may observe without fear of exaggeration, ran one of the strangest political systems ever invented. Praetorian guards who had seized power from a weak ruler, they perpetuated their control of the state, generation after generation, by buying slaves imported from the fringe-lands between the Caucasus and Turkey. Taken to Cairo, these young recruits were trained as Muslim warriors. The Mamelukes ruled Egypt ruthlessly, as conquered territory. Today's Turkish-speaking page might be tomorrow's *bey*, who, if he were handsome and skillful enough, might finally become sultan. Quarrelsome and extravagant, the Mamelukes nonetheless had their virtues and uses. Superb patrons of architecture, they endowed schools and hospitals. And their arms preserved Cairo—and, by extension, Mecca—from the fate of Baghdad.

To symbolize their sovereignty over Mecca, the Mamelukes contributed a striking innovation to the pageantry of pilgrimage: the annual dispatch from Cairo, along with the Kaaba's new covering, of an empty, closed pavilion swaying atop a splendid camel. The precise origin of the custom is disputed. The use of a *mahmal* to transport the *kiswa* may have devolved from early Arab practice, when a chief's daughter would ride in such a

state to incite warriors to battle. A romantic story associates the first use of the *mahmal* with a Mameluke queen, Shagrat al-Durr ("Tree of Pearls"), who had made the pilgrimage in person, concealed in a richly ornamented *mahmal*. Detained by business another year, she sent an empty *mahmal* instead, to symbolize her domination of the holy places. However this may be, it is certain that a few years later, in 1266, the great sultan Baibars sent an empty *mahmal* in state to Mecca—a political gesture designed to assert Egypt's protection of Islam's most important shrine.

The *mahmal*'s shape finds classical description in the prose of Edward Lane, who lived in early-nineteenth-century Cairo:

It is a square skeleton-frame of wood, with a pyramidal top; it has a covering of black brocade, richly worked with inscriptions and ornamental embroidery in gold, in some parts upon a ground of green or red silk, and bordered with a fringe of silk, with tassels surmounted by silver balls. Its covering is not always made after the same pattern, with regard to the decorations; but in every cover that I have seen, I have remarked, on the upper part of the front, a view of the Temple of Mekkeh, worked in gold; and, over it, the Sultán's cipher. It contains nothing; but has two mus-hafs (or copies of the Kur-án), one on a small scroll, and the other in the usual form of a book, also small, each enclosed in a case of gilt silver, attached externally at the top.

Lane also notes that the chosen camel, if it returned to Cairo, was given honorable retirement, richly fed, "and generously indulged with exemption from every kind of

With the collapse of the Abbasid dynasty in 1258, suzerainty over the Hijaz and Mecca was to pass to another foreign power, the Mamelukes of Egypt. For the next four centuries Mecca was held in the sway of one of the most curious political systems in all of human history—a military meritocracy, based in Cairo, that recruited its future leaders in the slave markets of Turkey and the Caucasus. Shifts in temporal power had little impact upon Meccan tourism, however, which continued unabated throughout the Mameluke era. Wealthy pilgrims arrived by sedan chair (left), but rich and poor alike donned traditional ihram *(right, below) for the* hajj *itself. A recurrent spectacle during this period was the dispatch, from Mameluke Cairo, of a* mahmal, *or empty, camel-borne pavilion—an annual reminder to Meccans of their subjugation.*

labour during the remainder of its life.''

After the Ottomans defeated the Mamelukes and occupied Egypt in 1517, they kept their foreign slaves as tax-collecting barons, subject to a pasha, or governor, from Constantinople. They also allowed the *mahmal* to make its yearly departure from below Cairo's citadel, where their pasha had his seat. By this time a second *mahmal* accompanied the great pilgrimage that, starting from Damascus, siphoned the Muslims of the Balkans, Anatolia, and Syria into a south-moving human stream. This *mahmal* would continue to symbolize the pilgrimage in the paintings found on peasant houses, even after the ideas and attitudes of the twentieth century led to abandonment of the *mahmal* itself.

An independent Arabia, aware of the link between the *mahmal* and foreign claims to sovereignty over Arab territory, forbade the arrival of the camel and its load in the 1920s. The stately contraption continued to leave Cairo intermittently—though not to go beyond Suez—until, after the Egyptian revolution of 1952, the Grand Mufti and the rector of al-Azhar University abolished it by decree. The reasons it was condemned are of some interest. The *mahmal* customarily made seven turns round a circle marked on the ground beneath the citadel, and this was held to be objectionable because circumambulation was only permissible at the Kaaba. Musicians and processions accompanied these turns, and this was said to affront the particular puritanism of revolution. The *amir al-hajj*, or prince of the pilgrimage, was accustomed to kiss the thigh of the camel, and this was deemed a pagan practice dating back to Queen Shagrat al-Durr, whose reputation was not of the purest. The ceremony was declared misleading to the faith-

Modern Mecca's Sacred Mosque owes it basic shape to the Abbasids, a Baghdad-based dynasty that put up the first great colonnade around the Kaaba. It owes its basic style, however, to the Ottomans, who ruled a sprawling Middle Eastern empire centered on Constantinople from the sixteenth century to the present one. As the visitor to Mecca is certain to note, the Sacred Mosque is actually two entirely separate structures: a six-inch gap, visible in the photograph at right, divides the older Ottoman arcades from the twentieth-century, Saudi-built colonnades (opposite) that now completely encircle them.

ful, giving them the false idea that these ceremonies were in some way Islamic. The ceremonies were also said to encourage manifestations by Sufi sheikhs and mystical brotherhoods.

Curiously enough, these mystical currents have effected changes in the role of Mecca and the Kaaba that go much deeper than additions to the mosque and other external alterations. They reflect a deepening attitude toward what the Kaaba represents. Muhammad himself is not generally accounted a mystic, although his Night Journey to the Seventh Heaven is more readily understood in mystical than literal terms. Yet the religion he revealed provided the structure for Sufism—a mystical school that was to influence Christian Europe through saints such as Teresa of Avila and John of the Cross, whose Spanish provenance made them aware of Islamic thought. And the Sufi attitude toward the Kaaba and the truths for which it stood lifted Islam far above pagan magic or legalistic conformism.

One of the greatest Sufi writers, ibn Arabi, was, like ibn Jubayr, a twelfth-century Spaniard. He visited Mecca in 1201, when he was thirty-six, and formed a spiritual attachment to a learned woman living in the holy city. She inspired him to compose a series of love poems that express, among other things, ibn Arabi's belief in the unity of all existence and the validity of all religions. Among 150 known works, ibn Arabi composed a vast compendium of mystical knowledge whose title, *Al-Futuhat al-Makiyya*, can be translated as *The Conquests of Mecca* or *The Revelations of Mecca*, depending on whether *Futuhat* is taken literally or metaphorically. The explosive nature of this masterpiece was demonstrated as recently as 1978, when the Egyptian parlia-

ment banned a thirty-six-volume edition of the work being published in Cairo by a Syrian scholar. Ibn Arabi, who has been denounced as a heretic or praised as a saint for the last seven centuries, had a vision of the youthful Jesus while visiting the Kaaba. He also proclaimed: "The true Kaaba is nothing other than our true selves."

In the same tradition another Sufi, Abu Yazid, wrote:

> On my first *hajj* I saw only the temple; the second time I saw both the temple and the Lord of the temple; and the third time I saw the Lord alone.

Classical pagan odes traditionally opened with the poet lamenting the lost encampment of his beloved. Using this idiom Abu Yazid wrote:

> The darkest thing in the world is the Beloved's house without the Beloved.

When the Kaaba became the symbol, not the reality, when its circumambulation acquired spiritual meaning, it banished the formalism that, by depending on a specific set of actions and words, led to dependence on guides. Without this symbolic enrichment the Kaaba could hardly have achieved its lasting hold over the deepest aspirations of so large a segment of mankind.

Exuberant ornamentation has always been the chief hallmark of Islamic architecture, and the Sacred Mosque in Mecca more than fulfills the first-time visitor's expectations in this regard. From its crenelated parapets and bas-relief-covered pediments (right) to its intricate brass grilles and its highly polished marble exterior walls (left), the enormous mosque's every architectural detail bespeaks its Muslim heritage. It is a style that compensates, through sheer variety, for what it lacks in cohesive design—and the results never fail to delight the visitor's eye. Where the great Gothic cathedrals of Western Europe achieve grandeur through repetition, the Sacred Mosque attains majesty through multiplicity. The core of the structure, for instance, is supported by hundreds of columns like the one below, each of them slightly different in shape and style.

VI

Mecca and Christendom

If we can picture a theologian from outer space, one able to speak terrestrial languages and disguise his alien nature, we can also picture him moving from church to mosque, asking those he encounters about their religious ideas. He would surely be struck by how much they shared. Both religions, he would discover, proclaim a single God who has revealed his moral law through a succession of envoys. Muslims and Christians alike exalt the virtues of justice, charity, and forgiveness. They believe that the extent to which they practice these virtues in life will largely determine their fate after death. At the same time, each faith encourages the ordinary, backsliding mortal by stressing that mercy is God's dominant quality. Yet if this cosmic visitor opened the history books in our public libraries he would as surely be struck by how often and how cruelly the adherents of Jesus and Muhammad have fought each other.

This is less surprising than it first seems. The Bible reports that the primal murder was of one brother by another, and history attests that the bitterest violence occurs between those with most in common. Sparta fought Athens to the point of mutual exhaustion, for example; and until the twentieth century, the history of France and England was a saga of wars. In this century Marxists of one stripe have reserved their fiercest hatreds for those of another. It is perhaps natural, therefore, that throughout the Middle Ages Islam seemed to be Christendom's most dangerous foe. (Dante, Europe's loftiest medieval poet, allows anal imagery to inform his portrait of the torments of Muhammad. Regarding the Prophet as a heretic and schismatic, Dante places him in the Ninth Circle of Hell in *The Divine Comedy*.) Politically, the two great religions split the Mediterranean, which had previously been a unifying sea. The Muslims termed their warmer world "the House of Peace" and dubbed Christendom "the House of War." In Spain and Italy, as in Anatolia—where the remnants of the Byzantine empire confronted a battered caliphate—the two faiths were parted by a medieval approximation of a free-fire zone. It was, nonetheless, an age that acknowledged a supreme moral law, and as a result brutality stopped short of twentieth-century standards. Chivalry—whose roots went back in part to pagan Arabia, in part to feudal Europe—generally prevented anything like total war.

From the point of view of Western European scholars of the Middle Ages, the gulf between Christian West and Islamic East was not only geographical but intellectual. And it placed them at a disadvantage, for at the time Islam was superior in both literature and science. Indeed, European scholars depended for their knowledge of what their own classical ancestors had written on Arabic translations that filtered north through Spain or Sicily. (Dante himself owed much to the Sufi poet ibn Arabi.) But because each religion had an absolute confidence in every comma of its creed or scripture, there was little ecumenical toleration for another group's beliefs. The Crusades marked the high tide of this intolerance, and they did produce brutality of the worst sort. It was a common thing, for example, for weary Crusaders to turn aside at some convenient ghetto on the road to Palestine and do their slaughtering there, without waiting until they had reached the Levant. One Crusade contented itself with sacking orthodox Constantinople, thereby weakening the Middle

Eastern Christians' resistance to the Muslim Turks. And when the Crusaders finally reached Jerusalem—the third holiest Islamic shrine because of its associations with Muhammad's Night Journey—they waded impartially through the blood of Muslims, Jews, and schismatic Christians.

By introducing such concepts as ambivalence, psychology has helped us to explain how contradictory emotions can be directed toward one and the same object, how an overt hatred can mask secondary attractions. Twelfth-century Europe, cut off from the outside world by Islam and the uncrossed Atlantic, was both fascinated and repelled by the East, where the followers of Muhammad ruled. And Mecca was the fascinating center of this mysterious, unapproachable, and hostile system. The adventures of Europeans who, managing to escape detection, visited the forbidden Kaaba and witnessed its rites form an epic of inventiveness, courage, and impudence. They also illuminate the shifting balance of power between the two civilizations, neither of which was aware of just how much it had in common with the other.

In medieval times, for example, no European city could rival Fatimid Cairo in size or luxury. On December 18, 1084, a visitor wrote in his diary that he had visited the central market and seen in the stalls jasmine, red roses, water lilies, narcissi, bitter and sweet oranges, lemons, apples, melons, bananas, fresh plums and dates, raisins, sugar cane, eggplant, zucchini, beets, turnips, celery, broad beans, cucumbers, onions, garlic, and carrots. The houses tended to be high, some having as many as fourteen stories, and the roofs supported terrace gardens. One householder had solved the problem of watering his rooftop paradise in an ingenious manner. He had taken a young calf onto the roof. In the course of time this beast had grown into a bull, and it was employed to turn an engine whose screws raised the water required for growing such useful plants as oranges and bananas as well as shrubs and flowers.

Islam's cultural superiority had long since declined when, in 1503, Ludovico Bartema visited Mecca. His native Italy, although politically as chaotic as the Middle East, was the recognized progenitor of the High Renaissance. The arts were fostered by pontiffs of outstanding taste, while science, though not yet fully free of the yoke of the Inquisition, was the enthusiasm of leading minds. The discovery that the world was round and that the Atlantic led to two previously unknown continents gave a new confidence to Europeans, no longer confined in their narrow peninsula. By contrast, the Islamic caliphate, devastated by the Mongol invasions of the thirteenth century, had recovered neither its power nor its unity.

In his account of his journey to Mecca, Bartema claims to have been motivated to make the trip by an "ardent desire of knowledge"—but his account shows him more interested in, and successful with, the opposite sex. Having reached Damascus, Bartema struck up a friendship with a certain "Captain Mameluke," and made the pilgrimage in his company. Bartema estimated the Syrian caravan at forty thousand men and thirty-five thousand camels—both plausible figures, although we have no means of checking their accuracy. The caravan was protected by an armed escort, and this proved fortunate since it was attacked by Bedouin marauders enroute. Bartema's impression of Mecca is less condescending than that of later European visitors. "The city is very fair and well inhabited," he notes, and, "contains in round form six thousand houses, as well built as ours, and some that cost three or four thousand pieces of gold: it has no walls." Bartema recognized in the mass slaughter of sheep, and the distribution of meat to the poor, a charity analogous to the practices of Christian Europe.

In 1517, fourteen years after Bartema's visit, Mameluke Egypt lost its independence to the Ottoman sultan Selim the Grim. The Ottoman Turks were to reunite the divided territories of the Middle East into the last major Islamic state, but only at the price of slow but steady deterioration. In the first decades of the sixteenth century the Ottoman empire ranked as the best organized, most militarily effective power in Europe, qualifying as a "European" power because it controlled most of the Balkan peninsula. But the Ottomans' disdain of commerce made them ill-equipped to confront a Europe whose commercial wealth and scientific innovations were to render it increasingly preeminent in the next two centuries.

The pendulum that would swing Europe into a position of superiority was already moving away from Islam when an English visitor left his impressions of Mecca as it was in the time of the last Stuart kings. Joseph Pitts went to Mecca under duress, as mentioned in an earlier chapter, rather than as the result of any particular wish. As a young sailor from Devonshire, he was captured by Algerian pirates who sold him into slavery. His master showed particular concern for his slave's salvation, converting Pitts to outward acceptance of the Prophet's re-

ligion by the continued application of a cudgel to his bare soles. (Such harshness, it should be noted, was typical of the times, and Pitts was to declare that his Muslim master behaved as a second father.) The pious master rewarded the English convert by taking him on the *hajj* to Mecca, where he gave Pitts his freedom. After a fifteen-year absence, Pitts was to make his way back to England, where he spent the rest of his life.

Pitts enables us to observe the frieze of Meccan life through the eyes of a contemporary of Daniel Defoe and William Penn. At Jiddah his party was met by "certain persons who came from Mecca on purpose to instruct the Hagges, or pilgrims, in the ceremonies (most of them being ignorant of them) which are to be used in their worship at the temple there; in the middle of which is a place which they call Beat Allah, i.e. the House of God. They say that Abraham built it; to which I give no credit." From these "guides" Pitts learned that the Black Stone had formerly been white and had acquired its black color "by reason of the sins of the multitudes of people who kiss it." He uses an unexpected adjective—"very ordinary"—to describe the buildings in Mecca, but his description of the people as very lean, thin, and swarthy is convincing. So too is his description of the landscape near Mecca, which, coming from someone who had left school at fifteen, is a tribute to the English educational system of his generation:

The town is surrounded for several miles with many thousands of little hills, which are very near one to the other. I have been on the top of some of them near Mecca, where I could see miles about.... They are all stony-rock and blackish, and pretty near of a bigness,

appearing at a distance like cocks of hay, but all pointing towards Mecca.

Pitts, in his simple style, also conveys what it was like to stay in the holy city:

> The inhabitants, especially men, do usually sleep on the tops of the houses for the air, or in the streets before their doors. Some lay the small bedding they have on a thin mat on the ground; others have a slight frame, made much like drink-stalls on which we place barrels, standing on four legs, corded with palm cordage, on which they put their bedding. Before they bring out their bedding, they sweep the streets and water them. As for my own part, I usually lay open, without any bed-covering, on the top of the house: only I took a linen cloth, dipt in water, and after I had wrung it, covered myself with it in the night; and when I awoke I should find it dry; then I would wet it again: and thus I did two or three times a night.

Inwardly, Pitts never forsook his English Christianity but, living before the pendulum had swung so far in Europe's favor that everything foreign could be dismissed as exotic or quaint, Pitts compares the Sacred Mosque to—of all things—the Royal Exchange in London. "But," he hastens to add, "I believe it is near ten times bigger."

During the hundred years that followed Pitts' pilgrimage, the Ottoman decline accelerated rapidly, a downward course marked by one defeat and one unfavorable treaty after another. The truly crucial shock to Islamic society, however, was Napoleon's arrival off Alexandria in 1798. His fleet carried an expeditionary force that included scholars and their instruments as well as soldiers with guns. On one level Napoleon was a military adventurer, and as an adventure his Egyptian expedition was thwarted when Lord Nelson's fleet caught and sank the French battle fleet in the Bay of Aboukir, some ten miles east of Alexandria. Although the French remained in occupation of Egypt for a few years thereafter, they were unable to reinforce their expedition without the fleet, and Napoleon was thus foiled in his strategic aim of separating the British from their empire in India.

On another, deeper level, Napoleon incarnated much of the spirit of the Enlightenment, and in this aspect his 1798 campaign played an unsettling yet stimulating role in Middle Eastern affairs. Through the agency of Napoleon's expedition Europe let loose on the now conservative world of Islam two contrasting forces. First, the amoral adventurism represented by Napoleon in his military aspect prompted charlatans, moneylenders, and thieves to seek their fortunes in an almost impotent East. Second, the high-minded idealism of the French academics who accompanied Napoleon—and who were followed, in their turn, by British, German, and American thinkers—revived the power to think and to react, much as Islam itself had shaken ecclesiastical Europe centuries before.

Napoleon the man of power actually inspired a local disciple, Muhammad Ali, a Macedonian Muslim, to follow a Westernizing course. Sent by the sultan to organize resistance to the French invasion, Muhammad Ali studied the situation in Egypt with a view to his own purposes. The once-creative Mameluke state was now a

The West has been in the business of "rediscovering" the Arab East for centuries, but never so impressively as in the late eighteenth century, when Napoleon Bonaparte launched his renowned 1798 expedition to the Middle East. As this Cruikshank cartoon, dubbed "Flight from Egypt," suggests, the French presence in the Levant was fleeting; their impact, on the other hand, was profound and enduring. Muhammad Ali, who succeeded the Mamelukes as ruler of Egypt and master of the Hijaz, did so by establishing a facsimile of French-style monarchy in nineteenth-century Cairo.

sluggish, underpopulated Ottoman province, misruled by Mameluke barons who saw no further than their parochial profit. In a famous coup, the new pasha invited the Mamelukes to a feast in the Citadel, shut the doors on them, and had them massacred. This enabled him to establish a pastiche of Western monarchy in Cairo, one virtually independent of Turkey, that lasted until the deposition of Muhammad Ali's great-great-grandson, King Farouk, in 1952.

Many of Muhammad Ali's leading officials were Europeans. Against such direct or indirect Western invasion, Islam was to produce its own resistance, headed sometimes by bigots, sometimes by reformers genuinely eager to put Islam on a sounder course. Even before Napoleon's arrival one such reformer, Muhammad Abdul Wahhab, had begun to preach, in the desert highlands of Central Arabia, a return to a simpler, purified religion. The Wahhabis, as the sect was known outside Arabia, described themselves by a term meaning "unitarians" and aimed to free Islam of later accretions. They managed to capture Islam's holy places from the Turks and hung the Kaaba with their own red *kiswa*. Muhammad Ali, on the sultan's orders, conducted a protracted campaign to clear the Wahhabis from the Hijaz. During his stay in Mecca, two Europeans managed to visit and describe the holy city as it then was. They represent two poles of nineteenth-century Western influence.

Ferrara-born Giovanni Finati dismissed the church training in which he was raised as a course of "frivolous and empty ceremonials and mysteries." Called to the colors in adolescence, he escaped military service with fifteen other Italian deserters by crossing the Adriatic to Muslim Albania, where he took the name Muhammad. Having already abandoned his country and his religion, he was to abandon, with charm, everyone he encountered. The Turkish general whom he served as pipe-bearer trusted him with the run of his house—which Finati saw as including the run of Fatima, his master's favorite Georgian wife. Fatima got pregnant and Finati fled to Alexandria, where he enlisted as an Albanian private soldier. Promoted to the rank of corporal in Muhammad Ali's bodyguard, he was present at the massacre of the Mamelukes in the Citadel.

Finati's next misadventure involved accidentally shooting his sergeant. To extract the turncoat Italian from this scrape, his commanding officer paid blood money to the dead man's family. Finati next found himself in the Hijaz. Involved in an Egyptian defeat at the hands of the Wahhabis, he had resolved to desert Muhammad Ali's army by the time he entered Mecca. This made him, he tells us, peculiarly responsive to strong impressions: "I was much struck with all I saw upon entering the city; for though it is neither large nor beautiful in itself, there is something in it that is calculated to impress a sort of awe, and it was the hour of noon when everything is very silent, except the Muezzins calling from the minarets."

What principally impressed "Muhammad" Finati, as reported by the Italian who ghosted his book, was

that celebrated sacred enclosure which is placed about the centre of it; it is a vast paved court with doorways opening into it from every side, and with a covered colonnade carried all round like a cloister, while in the midst of the open space stands the edifice called the

Kaaba, whose walls are entirely covered over on the outside with hangings of rich velvet, on which there are Arabic inscriptions embroidered in gold.

Finati's description, elsewhere, of the Kaaba as a "little square building" is, of course, inaccurate, since not one of its sides is the same length and its height exceeds its length and breadth. Nor was the *kiswa* made of velvet. This and other details such as the attribution of the place of sacrifice to Arafat, not Muna, make us suspect that Finati—who had a dread of circumcision, without which a visit to Mecca could be perilous—belonged to that class of adventurer who only pretended to scrutinize Mecca. (A sixteenth-century account by another visitor, the Frenchman Vincent Le Blanc, certainly reads like fiction.) What is surely genuine about Finati is the portrait he unconsciously presents of the kind of European who was to make his fortune in the Levant. "He was so ignorant," Sir Richard Burton, the noted Victorian traveler, declares, "that he had forgotten to write; his curiosity and his powers of observation keep pace with his knowledge; his moral character as it appears in print is of that description which knows no sense of shame: it is not candour but sheer insensibility which makes him relate circumstantially his repeated desertings, his betrayal of Fatimah, and his various plunderings." Yet it was men like Finati who later helped build modern Egypt and construct the Suez Canal. And their descendants were to compose the exotic diaspora literature memorably evoked in the poems of Constantine Cavafy and the prose of Lawrence Durrell's *Alexandria Quartet*.

Of different timber than Finati, and representative of a different aspect of the West, was John Lewis (Johann Ludwig) Burckhardt. He was not the first scientifically minded Westerner to visit Mecca, however; a Spaniard, Badia y Leblich, had preceded him, visiting the holy city during its takeover by the Wahhabis and before its reconquest by Muhammad Ali. "Ali Bey," as the Spaniard called himself, appreciated the spirit animating a crowd he estimated at more than eighty thousand:

> A countless crowd of men of all nations and colours come from the ends of the earth, through a thousand dangers, and fatigues without number, to worship together the same God. The inhabitant of the Caucasus gives a friendly hand to the Ethiopian or the Guinea Negro; the . . . Persian fraternises with the natives of Barbary and Morocco. All consider themselves members of one family. There is no intermediary between man and his God; all are equal before their creator.

Ali Bey's sympathy for the East may explain the rumor that he was a Catalonian Jew—or may be explained by it. We know he traveled in state, with access to mysterious funds, and we suspect that he was working for French intelligence. In any event he had a gift for the striking phrase. For instance, a much decayed Mecca, its population down to a fifth of what it had been in caliphal times, seemed to him "muffled in its deserts like a sick man from the noises of the outer world."

Burckhardt's approach to Islam was that of the devoted scholar. Leipzig and Göttingen, then Cambridge and London, prepared the young Swiss for what he planned would be a series of exploratory journeys to little-visited tracts of Africa and the Near East. He left England

"Mecca abounds with rogues, who are tempted by the facility of opening the locks of this country," reported the Swiss adventurer John Lewis Burckhardt from Mecca in 1814. Burckhardt, who gained entrance to the holy city by adopting both the dress and language of the natives. Burckhardt's complaint was not original when he raised it, and it has been echoed by uncounted travelers since his time. Rank opportunists have been turning the neophyte hajji's ignorance of hajj ritual to their advantage since time immemorial—and their scavenging persists to this day. Indeed, one of the tasks facing the new Hajj Research Centre in Jiddah is that of developing an effective means of policing the profiteers who swarm over Mecca during the pilgrimage season. The stalls that line the city's narrow streets offer the faithful a wide range of overpriced comestibles (above), which the pilgrim generally cannot avoid purchasing, and a bewildering variety of souvenirs—-Korans bound in leather (left), brightly colored posters (right), and water from Zemzem, the holy city's sacred well (top right).

101

in 1809 for Aleppo, where he studied Arabic. As evidence of his linguistic genius—or, perhaps, of the low level of learning among the Arabs he met—he could apparently convince "the most learned Mussulmans that he was a learned doctor of their law." Burckhardt actually passed himself off as Sheikh Ibrahim ibn Abdullah, and after a visit to Nubia in 1812 he was ready to perform the pilgrimage in 1814. This bold project was made easier by the fact that Muhammad Ali, whom he had met in Cairo, was then in occupation of the holy city and, accustomed to being surrounded by so many adventurers, had no desire to pry into the young man's identity. Imposture seemed to be part of the travelers' role: Burckhardt sometimes pretended to be British, and he claims that many genuine pilgrims were equally deceptive about their country of origin. Where Burckhardt did not invent was in his approach to his material, which was inclusive and accurate. On the people he is objective, balancing virtues with vices:

> The Makkawys, like the inhabitants of Turkey, are in general free from the vices of pilfering and thieving; and robberies are seldom heard of, although, during the Hadj, and in the months which precede and follow it, Mekka abounds with rogues, who are tempted by the facility of opening the locks of this country.

Bedouin generosity, he notes, was not extinct:

> There is a great politeness without formality; and no men appear in a more amiable light, than the great Mekkawys dispensing hospitality to their guests. Whoever happens to be sitting in the outer hall, when dinner is served up, is requested to join at table, which he does without conceiving himself at all obliged by the invitation while the host, on his part, appears to think compliance a favour conferred upon him.

Yet he observes the mercenary taint attaching to religious tourism: "All Mekka seems united in the design of cheating the pilgrims." And this, he feels, led to a lack of culture. "Learning and science cannot be expected to flourish in a place where every mind is occupied in the search of gain, or of paradise," he observes, "and I think I have sufficient reason for affirming that Mekka is at present much inferior even in Mohammedan learning to any town of equal population in Syria or Egypt."

At the time of Burckhardt's pilgrimage, no public school offered lectures, and no houses, except for the mosque and a few mansions belonging to the Sharif, impressed. Burckhardt is precise on figures, naming the guides as eight hundred, with many boy apprentices. More than forty eunuchs, gifts of pashas and grandees who gave each a hundred dollars for his outfit, served the mosque. Muhammad Ali himself had presented the mosque with ten such doctored youths.

This modest, self-effacing writer perished of a fever in Cairo in 1817, before he could complete a visit to the Fezzan in southwest Libya. His *Travels in Arabia* were published by a learned society in London twelve years after his death.

A generation later, as the British empire approached its plateau of power and expansion, Mecca received its most flamboyant Western visitor. The name Mirza Abdullah and the clothes of a Persian darwish, or wander-

Burckhardt's account of life in Mecca is not the most famous or the most frequently read, but it is in many ways the most detailed, balanced, and reliable. Consequently, the posthumous record of his travels in which this map of the Plains of Arafat appeared is more sober and less flattering than most in its assessment of nineteenth-century Mecca—which Burckhardt felt compelled to dismiss as "inferior even in Mohammedan learning to any town of equal population of Syria or Egypt."

ing holy man, concealed Sir Richard Burton, a British military officer whose Indian Army career had been blighted when his voluminous notes on the low life of Karachi inadvertently found their way into the hands of a humorless superior. In some moods Burton probably felt himself to be Muslim, but his approach to the journey was that of an actor, not a pilgrim. He spent a fortnight in Alexandria, noting and imitating Eastern manners—and making entries in his journal:

> Look, for instance, at that Indian Moslem drinking a glass of water. With us the operation is simple enough, but his performance includes no fewer than five novelties. In the first place he clutches his tumbler as though it were the throat of a foe; secondly, he ejaculates, "In the name of Allah the Compassionate, the Merciful!" before wetting his lips; thirdly, he imbibes the contents, swallowing them, not sipping them as he ought to do, and ending with a satisfied grunt; fourthly, before setting down the cup, he sighs forth, "Praise be to Allah!"—of which you will understand the full meaning in the Desert; and, fifthly, he replies, "May Allah make it pleasant to thee!"

Stanley Lane-Poole, a Victorian orientalist, characterized Burton's account of Mecca as a "compound of keen observation, wide Oriental learning, a grim sardonic humour, and an insobriety of opinion expressed in the writer's vigorous vernacular." Burton's pseudo-Elizabethan vernacular strikes most modern readers as fustian, but it typifies a period when the East was investigated or enjoyed but hardly taken seriously in its own right. Burton, at odds with Victorian morality, was sti-

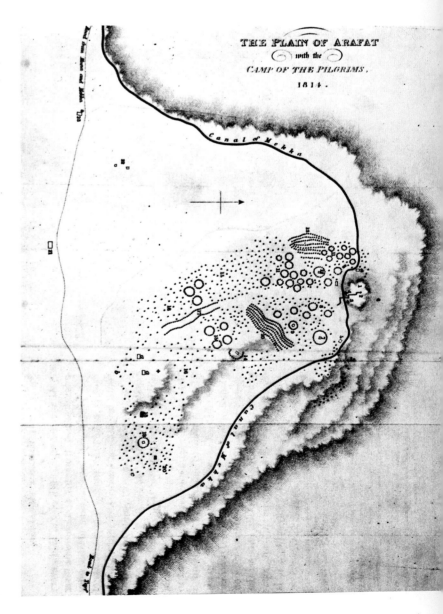

THE PLAIN OF ARAFAT with the CAMP OF THE PILGRIMS. 1814.

The tragedy of Burckhardt's early death was to be compounded, a decade later, by the arrival in Mecca of Sir Richard Burton—a Victorian so eminent that his **Pilgrimage to Al-Madinah and Meccah** *promptly eclipsed Burckhardt's account and became the standard source for information about Mecca and Arabia. This subsequent generations would come to regret, for Burton's book was neither as carefully researched nor as well written as his predecessor's, yet it served for decades as the definitive assessment of Islamic culture. Burton, who was far more imposing than this 1885 caricature makes him out to be, completed the* hajj *in the garb of a Persian holy man and, thus disguised, witnessed the ritual casting of stones that is an aspect of the* hajj. *Opposite, an illustrator's rendering of the rite from Burton's own book.*

fled by his marriage to a devoted but conventional wife. Lady Burton was eventually to bury her idolized husband in a marble tomb modeled on an Arab tent, complete with camel-bells. She was also to burn those of his manuscripts that shocked her sensibility.

As a man whose complex, often neurotic interests made him a pioneer sexologist—a development that prevented him from becoming more than a consul in the imperial service—Burton is undervalued. But as a travel writer he may be overvalued; his account of Mecca, for all its diverting details, cannot rival Burckhardt's calm objectivity. Burton implicitly concedes this by reprinting, in his own *Pilgrimage to Al-Madinah and Meccah* (1855), the thirty pages in which Burckhardt described the Sacred Mosque.

Yet though Burckhardt and Burton differed in style and temperament, they were as one in believing that the *hajj* would diminish in importance or come under Western tutelage. "The time had passed, and probably forever," wrote Burckhardt, "when hadjys or pilgrims, from all regions of the Muslim world, came every year in multitudes, that they might visit devotionally the sacred places of the Hadjaz." He attributed this to an increasing indifference to religion and the rising costs of travel. Burckhardt, a child of the French Revolution, might logically have assumed that such rites would wither in the rays of scientific advance. Burton, for all his attraction to the picturesque and wild, saw diminu-

tion of a different kind: "It requires not the ken of a prophet," he wrote as he planned further expeditions to Abyssinia and the sources of the Nile, to foresee the day when political necessity—that sternest of necessities—"will compel us to occupy in force the fountainhead of Al-Islam."

For all their dressing up as natives, both the German-Swiss and the English aristocrat proud of his Gypsy heritage felt that they were living in the twilight of Islam. They were certainly living at a time when curiosity about Mecca as the mysterious center of an antagonistic culture had yielded to sociological concern. This served the imperial ambitions of the European powers, one of which would soon feel "compelled" to occupy—and, by implication, civilize—Islam's most sacred site. Burckhardt and Burton alike imagined the future in terms of Western rule. And they were not alone in this imperialistic view: Edward W. Said, a stern critic of orientalism and its motives, has reminded us that Karl Marx shared a similar belief. "England has to fulfill a double mission in India," wrote the author of *Das Kapital*, in words that he might equally have applied to the Middle East, "one destructive, the other regenerating—the annihilation of the Asiatic society, and the laying of the material foundations of Western society in Asia."

In the struggle between this view and the one held by those on the receiving end of Western imperialistic designs, Mecca would play an incalcuable role.

VII

Mecca and an Embattled Islam

In 1817, the year Burckhardt died, the English poet Percy Bysshe Shelley, who never visited the Middle East, was at work on *The Revolt of Islam*. A narrative poem dedicated to the transience of error and the eternity of genius and virtue, it had little to do with Islamic realities. Its strange title was ultimately prophetic, although, in the short run, the upsurge Shelley's title evokes consisted of revolts by subjugated nation-states determined to break free of Islam—not by an Islam determined to rid itself of the imperialist powers. Lord Byron, Shelley's fellow Romantic and friend, died in 1824, a fevered martyr to the cause of Greek independence. And similar revolts against the Ottoman sultan were to culminate, a hundred years later, in the formal abolition of the sultan-caliphate.

A Europe eager to share in the sultanate's rich spoils discovered, in nationalism, a weapon more powerful than rifles or gold sovereigns. What had once been a progressive aspect of Islamic statecraft—the concept that varied religious groups could live together under the sultan's rooftree—now seemed anachronistic and tyrannical. The concept was indeed old, going back as it did to the practices of the Prophet himself. After the surrender of Khaybar oasis, for instance, its Jewish inhabitants were allowed to cultivate the land as before—on condition they paid a regular tax to the coffers of the state that would henceforth protect them. In Khaybar's case this lofty principle soon clashed with another, namely that Jews were not allowed to live within the Hijaz. Outside the sacred province, however, Jews and Christians were to conduct their religious affairs under leaders answerable to the Muslim authorities.

This system was not ideal, since in effect it distin-guished a first-class and a second-class citizenry, but it was more generous than the practice then current virtually everywhere else—which was that anyone who did not adhere to the majority faith suffered the constant risk of persecution. In the sixteenth century, when Europe's feuding states were testing their citizens' beliefs through various species of Inquisition, the Ottomans seemed so comparatively tolerant that the migration of peoples seeking refuge from religious persecution was into the sultan's realms, not out of them. When, for instance, Ferdinand and Isabella expelled non-Christians from a reconquered Spain, many Iberian Jews traveled the length of the Mediterranean to settle in Smyrna and Salonika. As subjects of the sultan they could practice Judaism in relative safety—and also find outlets for their professional skills. The same was true for many Christians. The Greek Orthodox clergy of Cyprus, for example, preferred the turban of the sultan to the tiara of the Pope, represented on their island by Western Europeans who had installed themselves as a feudal aristocracy. The Armenians, whose Christianity differed in its details from that of Greek Orthodoxy—and who had suffered during the border wars between Byzantium and Persia—were known, after their absorption into the Ottoman empire, as "the faithful nation" and were widely employed in administration and finance.

This situation, whose virtues should be appreciated but not exaggerated, changed with the French Revolution and the new political thinking it engendered. In the mid-sixteenth century, under Suliman the Magnificent, the Turkish army had been the most effective in Europe; by 1798 its decline was conspicuous. Such politically subordinate groups as Greeks, Bulgars, and

Serbs no longer desired to remain inside a technological backwater presided over by an absolute sultan. They had long seen themselves as religious communities presided over by patriarchs or ethnarchs; now they began to see themselves as nations in the Western sense—that is, as groups sharing a culture, language, and imagined ethnic homogeneity. As such, they felt they had an inalienable right to territorial independence.

The spread of such ideas facilitated the dismemberment of the Ottoman sultanate—to the immediate advantage of Europe. Where provinces were not detached from the empire by the revolts of peoples willing to accept Western—usually German—kinglets, large regions were taken over by summary occupation, with the Ottoman ruler replaced by a colonial governor. France was to seize Algeria, Tunisia, and finally Morocco in this fashion, and Great Britain employed various pretexts to prolong into the 1950s an occupation of Egypt declared "temporary" in 1882.

During this period Mecca and what it represented became vitally important to the Ottoman state. In their military heyday its sultans had hardly bothered with the title of Caliph—which, in the strictest sense, could only be properly held by an Arab descended from the Prophet's tribe, the Koraysh. The Ottomans, whose male ancestors had come from Central Asia, had no such kinship claim. But as outsiders began to drive wedges into the empire's structure, the religious cement of Islam became the more essential. It could not bind to Constantinople the hearts of Christians, but it could exert a hold over the sultan's Muslim subjects—who included, besides the Turks, such important groups as the Arabs and the Kurds.

A Dutchman who lived in Mecca at the end of the nineteenth century noted that pilgrims from Indonesia, then ruled by Holland, arrived docile, but went home firebrands. The *hajji*, always respected on religious grounds, had become a disseminator of revolt. One skeikh told the Dutchman, who had passed himself off as a Muslim, that back in his native Java hundreds visited him nightly to ask "if the time were at hand, and how long the Kafir government could continue." The word *kafir* had originally meant infidel; long before the nineteenth century it had come to mean non-Muslim. Indonesians used it against the all-powerful Dutch as a means of verbal attack—much as the Dutch would later use it in South Africa against the blacks.

The advance of European industrialization increased the threat to the embattled sultan. He could see no limit to Europeans' ambitions as their railways moved to his frontiers and their ships steamed his seas. He might regard the loss of Greece, Bulgaria, or Serbia as painful but not lethal amputations; he could not be equally philosophical about secessionist stirrings by Armenians or Arabs. The Armenians were by this time dispersed in the major cities of the empire as well as in eastern Anatolia, and the savageries inflicted on them, in many ways rivaling the genocidal atrocities of modern tyrants, can be explained—although never excused—as a panicky response to an independence movement that could only succeed by destroying Turkey.

Arab secession would be equally perilous, for it would undermine the whole *raison d'être* of this last Islamic empire. The theory of Arab nationalism was propagated from Beirut, open as it was to Western missionaries, and its proponents were largely Christians. It

was patronized, with some qualifications, by the French, who had their eyes on Syria, and by the British, whose attitude to the Ottoman empire had changed radically from support, as shown by their alliance with the Turks in the Crimean War, to suspicion, as the last great sultan, Abdul Hamid, developed increasingly friendly ties with imperial Germany.

The Turkish interest in the Arabs, an interest focused on Mecca, was political and strategic, not economic. The sultan's claim to be Caliph not only held his own empire together but could be used against the French and British, who ruled millions of Muslim subjects. In this sense Islam provided inspiration for resistance from the Dutch East Indies to darkest Africa. In the Sudan, a Muslim with messianic tendencies, the Mahdi, led the first successful revolt against Western imperialism. And in thinly populated Libya an Italian occupation begun just before World War I encountered fierce resistance from the Senussis, tribesmen sustained in their rebellion by a mystical form of Islamic faith. (Among the Turkish officers who aided the Libyan resistance was the future rebuilder of a secular Turkey: Mustafa Kemal, later surnamed Atatürk.) Suzerainty over Arab lands gave Turkey access to Asia and Africa, two of the three continents across which her dominions sprawled. Economically, the Arab provinces seemed irretrievably poor, for the nineteenth century ran on coal and the extent of Arab oil wealth was not yet suspected. It is of interest, however, that when the founder of modern Zionism, Theodor Herzl—who was trying to obtain Palestine from the sultan as a homeland for the Jews—met Abdul Hamid, the latter remarked that he had just had a cable from Baghdad announcing the dis-

The systematic dismemberment of the Ottoman empire was so protracted and so well-publicized that long before the operation was over the world's press had taken to calling Turkey "the Sick Man of Europe." In most instances the scalpel was wielded by the sultan's own subjects—conspicuous among them the Greeks, Bulgars, and Serbs—but their separatist movements were openly encouraged by the Great Powers, who saw in the moribund Turkey (below) an opportunity for imperial aggrandizement unrivaled since the "opening" of China to Western trade earlier in the nineteenth century. Most avid to clutch the Sick Man in its ursine embrace was tsarist Russia (right), whose age-old dream of a warm-water port seemed suddenly closer to fulfillment. By 1896, when famed illustrator Sir John Tenniel executed the cartoon opposite, Turkey had in fact been "reorganized" by the Great Powers.

covery of a rich oil field.

The Ottomans, perceptive observers of their own decline, read widely and wrote at length on how that decline might be reversed. To give their state a rigid corset of law they codified the Sharia, or Holy Law. To improve their armed forces they bought modern weapons from Britain and Germany. They even risked putting their military secrets at the disposal of enemies by inviting one mission from Britain to train their navy and another from Prussia to provide the same service for their army. (The effects of this training were to become evident less than two decades later, during World War I, when the Turks defeated an Allied expeditionary force that tried to seize the Gallipoli Peninsula at the entrance to the Dardanelles.) But perhaps most imaginatively, the Ottomans planned to link their vulnerable provinces by a network of rail. In particular, they planned two gigantic steel prongs, one of which would link Constantinople—and the connecting railway to Germany—with Baghdad and the Persian Gulf; the other would make it possible to travel from the imperial capital to the birthplace of the Prophet by way of the caliphal capital of Damascus.

This latter line, the Hijaz Railway, was one of the marvels of the Age of Steam. It can rightfully claim a place alongside such projects as the tsarist Transiberian Railway or the Suez and Panama canals. Its creation was received with rapture by the Islamic masses, who were well aware of how little of Islam was still free of *kafir* rule, and how much of that was under threat. The railway was funded by public subscription, and for once an Ottoman public works project was executed without the customary corruption.

The Hijaz was the one place in all Islam that did not greet the new project with unmarred delight. The Muslim holy land had been under Ottoman sovereignty since the defeat of the Mamelukes in the early sixteenth century, but its isolation had left it relatively untouched. A dynasty of Hashemite sharifs, claiming descent from Muhammad Ali's second son, Hassan, held suzerainty over the Hijaz in 1901, when the railway was begun. They were divided into two hostile factions, but they shared a common desire to control a fiefdom as free of Turkish supervision as possible. The coming of the railway to Medina and then Mecca would effectively destroy, in a single blow, the Hijaz's last defense against Turkish meddling—its barren isolation.

At this time the Hashemites, Ottoman by education, ruled Mecca in ramshackle state. Hedley Churchward, a British actor who became a Muslim, visited the Sharif's palace and described it as looking "extremely plain from outside, with bare rows of windows." The premises, he observed, resembled nothing so much as a large factory. Churchward also recorded his impressions of the Turkish army of occupation: soldiers in ragged uniforms, "laughing, good-natured Anatolians, Kurds, Druses and other queer tribesmen." The Hashemites saw in these soldiers a menace to their power, and this gave them common ground, which they might otherwise have lacked, with the marauding Bedouin, who saw the railway as a threat to their livelihood.

In subsidizing adventurers like Burckhardt and Burton, such institutions as the Royal Geographic Society spent their money wisely. In the late nineteenth and early twentieth centuries British army intelligence on the Middle East was detailed and accurate. Its headquarters was Cairo, where the British ruled through a puppet monarchy—and the unrest in the Hijaz soon came to the attention of Lord Kitchener, the consul-general in Cairo. Sharif Hussein sent his astute second son, Abdullah, to call on Kitchener just before the outbreak of World War I. The visit was not without irony, for Kitchener had recently used a railway and armed gun-trains to reconquer the Sudan from the Mahdi.

The British agent was guarded in his responses to Abdullah, for his government was still on friendly terms with Turkey and hoped that if war did break out between Germany and Britain the sultan would at least remain neutral. At the same time Kitchener and his secretary for Oriental affairs, Ronald Storrs, let the Sharif understand that in the event of war between Britain and Turkey, an armed uprising in the Hijaz would not go unsupported. There were important considerations for Britain. Trouble in Arabia would force the Turks to withdraw troops from the border with Egypt and from the Balkans, while a revolt led by so prestigious a figure as the Sharif—and launched from the most holy place in Islam—would do much to offset the damage of an Ottoman call to *jihad*, or holy war.

Turkey was indeed to declare *jihad* in late 1914. Her entry into the war on the side of Germany was prompted by emotional factors and was disastrous for her own ultimate interests. Britain had agreed to supply Turkey with two modern warships, paid for, like the railway, by public subscription. With the outbreak of war, Britain simply transferred the completed ships to her own navy. Several months later, in one of his few inspired diplomatic moves, the kaiser sent two German replacements, which managed to penetrate the British naval

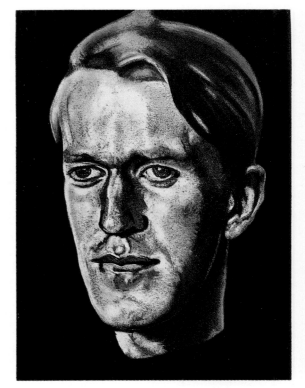

blockade and lower anchor in the Golden Horn. In a brilliant public relations gesture the German sailors changed their flat naval caps for the Ottoman fez.

Turkey had backed what what would prove to be the losing side, and in 1916 the Sharif openly supported the British. While the Turks clung stubbornly to the railhead of the Hijaz line in Medina, only surrendering it after the armistice of 1918, Mecca fell to the sharifian forces in the first days of the revolt. For the first time since the seventh century, the holy city was an independent capital. King Hussein, as the Sharif now called himself, had a military band composed of Turkish prisoners of war and a telephone number: Mecca 1. He relied for officers on deserters from the Ottoman army and for his soldiers on Arab tribesmen. For arms—and money with which to subvert the tribes still loyal to the sultan-caliph—he was totally dependent on the British, who appointed a number of political officers to guide the Arab revolt against the hated Turks along lines acceptable to London. Among these was T. E. Lawrence, who was to become an enigmatic, legendary hero in the postwar world.

Although Hussein was sincere in his espousal of Arab nationalism, his dependence on two *kafir* countries, Britain and France, made him suspect among most Arabs, particularly in light of the openly imperialistic ambitions of these two Western powers. The largely non-Arab townsfolk of Mecca showed no enthusiasm for the revolt, and Lawrence on one occasion estimated its support among the Bedouin as around 2 per cent. Hussein's already tenuous position was irretrievably weakened in 1917 when the new Bolshevik government revealed that the Sharif's British patrons—whom he had seen as committed to pan-Arab freedom—had made contradictory promises, both to the French (who were to receive a mandate over Syria and Lebanon) and to the Zionists (who were offered a national home in Palestine by the Balfour Declaration of 1917).

The man whom Lawrence had personally selected as the best figurehead for the revolt was Abdullah's younger brother, the Emir Feisal. Feisal entered Damascus at the head of a detachment of Arab troops in October 1918, but real power lay with the British general, Sir Edmund Allenby, whose non-guerilla army had fought the Turks north through Palestine. Four hundred years of Ottoman domination had ended. For a short period Feisal ruled in his father's name over a liberated Syria, but despite his attendance with Lawrence at the Versailles Peace Conference, he was soon forced to accept the realities of French control and flee his kingdom. It is possible that King Hussein might have held on to his own limited Kingdom of the Hijaz had he been willing to accept British conditions as spelled out to him by Lawrence, who visited him in Jiddah in the summer of 1921. At this time Lawrence was serving as adviser to Winston Churchill, Colonial Secretary in Prime Minister David Lloyd George's postwar cabinet. Hussein was bluntly told that he could expect an annual subsidy of £100,000 and a guarantee against a powerful neighbor, the Wahhabi leader ibn Saud, so long as he accepted Britain's general policy for the Middle East. Besides a French mandate over Syria and Lebanon and a British mandate over Iraq, this included the Balfour Declaration, already accepted by Hussein's second son, Abdullah, who was to prove a more compliant figure than his father. On the question of Palestine Hussein refused to yield, however, arguing that its population was 90 per cent Arab and refusing to accept as genuine the declaration's stipulations that the concession to the Jews would not be at the expense of the Arabs.

Hussein's refusal was to cost him his throne—and Mecca its brief moment of prestige as a capital city. The king might have raised funds adequate to administer a state as simple as that of Yemen to the south, but the Hijaz was not Yemen and he could not survive militarily without a British guarantee. Hussein and his family, who lacked popular support even in their own capital, were also paying the price, in terms of morale, for the long centuries in which the Meccans had lived by the religious tourist trade. Hussein was probably the only member of his family to be activated by principle; his other male relations were prepared to make sweeping concessions in return for political and financial survival.

Arabians of a very different order were mustering to the east under a remarkable new leader, a descendant of the movement that had tried, in the time of Muhammad Ali, to seize Mecca and Medina and purify them of abuses. Abdul Aziz ibn Saud, the founder of Saudi Arabia, had created a fighting force, the *Ikhwan*, or Brothers, who took to the battlefield with a zeal to match that of the first fighters for Islam. While the Hashemites of Mecca appealed to British romantics, impressed by pedigrees going back to the Prophet, inscrutable providence had conferred vitality on the Saudis.

The British made one or two additional efforts to persuade Hussein to accept the role of a puppet. Failing in this, they abandoned him to his fate. Defeated in engagement after engagement by the Saudi forces, Hussein abdicated in 1924 in favor of his eldest son,

Ali, who fled the Hijaz a few months later. In the same year Hussein made one last desperate move to regain a role in Middle Eastern affairs. Turkey had just announced, belatedly, the abolition of the caliphate, and Hussein had himself declared Commander of the Faithful, the age-old synonym for Caliph, by his son Abdullah in Amman. But this claim was hardly taken seriously outside his family circle, and with his bid for titular glory reduced to little more than a historical footnote, the old man moved to exile in Cyprus. His eldest son moved to Baghdad, where Lawrence's favorite, Feisal, had been compensated with the throne of Iraq.

Mecca, for a few years the capital of a state that had issued postage stamps designed by T. E. Lawrence and Ronald Storrs, was now occupied by the *Ikhwan*. Its royal palace looted of its archives, its lax morality replaced by a literal application of Koranic law, Mecca was subjected to a moral and physical clean-up that affected almost all aspects of the city's life. The Mecca from which Hussein had fled was an impoverished city whose public buildings combined provincial lethargy with Ottoman charm. In part because of that poverty and provincialism, Mecca had maintained a continuity of style and custom hardly rivaled elsewhere. Under the rule of a desert dynasty who brought with them a puritanical faith—and who soon acquired an income beyond the dreams of Midas—Muhammad's holy city was to upset the standard expectations of the orientalist and the Oriental in less than fifty years. A religion regarded as ossified was suddenly to become a revolutionary force, and a rite regarded as moribund was to attract pilgrims in excess of two million annually to the "barren valley" named in the Koran.

The English artist responsible for both of the portraits on the preceding spread fleshed out his gallery of faces familiar to all those with a knowledge of contemporary Arabia with depictions of three key figures in modern Meccan history. They are: Sharif Hussein (right), who led the rebels of the Hijaz against the sultan; his son Feisal (top right), whom Lawrence of Arabia was to personally choose to lead the figurehead government in Damascus; and his politically astute son Abdullah (above), whose willingness to comply with the Balfour Declaration as he understood it ensured his short-term political survival—and led to his eventual assassination. It was Hussein's refusal to accept the Declaration that cost him his throne—and Mecca, its passing position as capital of the newly formed nation.

VIII

Mecca in the Age of Oil

Pilgrims to Mecca in the late twentieth century may expect surprises. For one thing, the predictions made by their Western predecessors, valued as both balanced and brilliant a century ago, are visibly confuted. In the year of Napoleon's fall, for instance, Burckhardt gave Islam, a religion of the torrid zones, little future in an age dominated by northern science. Yet, rather than dwindling, the numbers participating in the *hajj* have actually multiplied—from thousands in Burckhardt's time to some two million today. Similarly, Sir Richard Burton, who was secretly attracted to the virtues and vices of the East, accepted the notion that Mecca would become another item in the White Man's Burden. As we know, this functionary of empire was as wrong as the Swiss-German rationalist: today an Arab state with unprecedented financial wealth and political influence is the guardian of the Sacred Mosque in Mecca and the Prophet's Mosque in Medina.

Quite apart from these essentially political considerations, Mecca itself may well confound imaginations nourished in childhood on legends of the traditional *hajj*. Most modern pilgrims arrive by air, having entered *ihram* before boarding their flight. Air-conditioned buses rush them from the Red Sea coast to hotels that, except for the absence of bars and nightclubs, offer the same services as their counterparts in Rome or Buenos Aires. Ended are the forty-day treks across the desert, with huge caravans moving in the cool of the evening and great flares burning in metal holders on the end of poles. Camels and horses no longer move through the darkness to the chant of prayers. A packaged religious tour, an instant pilgrimage, is all too likely. Mecca, in a word, sums up the opportunities, the problems, and the

vulgarities of an age in which money has exploded like a cloudburst on the Island of the Arabs.

On the other hand, our ecumenical age is more ready to look upon Mecca not as a religious curiosity but as a potential spiritual powerhouse. In the Age of Steam, by contrast, few Westerners questioned the authority or canons of Europe. Consider David G. Hogarth, who was not only the spymaster of T. E. Lawrence but also a competent historian of the exploration of Arabia. In his writings he belittles the art of ancient Egypt, comparing it most unfavorably with that of Greece. This attitude, often supported by some specious theory of racial inequality, reflected the consensus of the age.

As it happened, Hogarth served as Keeper of Oxford's Ashmolean Museum, which, like similar institutions all over the Western world, deposited its Benin bronzes, Ashanti masks, and Polynesian totems in dusty cellars. Like the Kaaba, these "primitive" artifacts interested the specialist in outlandish customs, but they were not considered works of art worthy to be discussed with, say, the Elgin Marbles or the paintings of Watteau. The religion of Muhammad was similarly studied, often by missionaries, in an ethnological context. It was valued because it was perceived to give stamina to such colonial levies as the Pathans of British India or the Zouaves of North Africa; it was criticized for its supposed suppression of women and then damned for its alleged fanatical component once Muslims began resisting Western rule. Those who wanted to study its source, in Mecca, prepared themselves by miming Arab gestures and dyeing their faces brown.

These elastic but tensile attitudes concerning the non-European world, shared by men as diverse in their

thinking as Marx and Kipling, were to be ravaged like a spider's web by twentieth-century gales. These high winds of chance tore rents in European power and self-confidence alike. First came World War I, which accomplished the destruction of the Ottoman empire, laying its Arabic provinces open to colonization and exploitation. But the war to end war also felled such proud dynasties as the Hohenzollerns of Germany, the Habsburgs of Austria-Hungary, and the Romanovs of tsarist Russia. Britain and France, the nominal victors, were entitled to enlarge their dominions with the colonial equivalent of adipose tissue, but they too shared in the collective weakening of European power.

In 1914, at the outbreak of the war, the territories sending pilgrims to Mecca were largely controlled by Britain, France, Holland, Italy, and Spain. The *hajji* from Algiers, Lahore, or Jakarta received his travel documents from Western officials, who put him in quarantine if he was suspected of carrying disease. Proconsuls like Lord Cromer, who ruled Egypt for Britain, and Marshal Lyautey, who ruled Morocco for France, died convinced that, plans preparing their regions for self-government notwithstanding, Western domination of Arabia should be maintained for centuries.

By the end of World War II in 1945, these assumptions had wilted. A new world organization, the United Nations, based in New York City, included more than a hundred formerly dependent territories, from three continents, as sovereign states. Algeria and South Yemen won their freedom by armed revolt, and many other Muslim lands received theirs from a war-weary West aware that this second international storm had blown down the scaffold of its power. By the 1960s most of the pilgrims who went to Mecca did so with documents issued by independent authorities—in Arabic or in other Third World tongues.

Significant as these developments were, it was an internal revolution in Western attitudes toward the Middle East that was ultimately to prove more important than the external changes signified by new passports and postage stamps. This shift in the West's approach to non-European cultures had actually begun before World War I. Some historians date it from the winter of 1906–07 when Picasso created *Les Demoiselles d'Avignon* in Paris. This disturbing masterpiece depicted young women in terms of Congolese masks, and it represented a brutal defiance of European artistic tradition. A new openness to non-Western modes of expression, led by pioneers like Picasso, brought increasing recognition that objects hitherto valued only for their folkloric interest also had aesthetic merit. And this certainly applied to Islam. The fussily intricate decoration of damascene ceilings and boxes had long appealed to Western tourists, but the essence of Islamic art—at its most memorable in the grand if sometimes bleak congregational mosques of Cairo, Istanbul, and India—was linked to a genius for abstraction, the legecy of nomadic forebears who lived under a vast desert sky, broken only by the stars.

This abstract quality in Islamic art revealed itself in the mode of decoration known as arabesque, in the massive Kufic calligraphy of early inscriptions, and, scientifically, in the symbolic language of algebra. (Compared to Western religious buildings the Kaaba was as geometric as a pyramid.) An affinity with this aspect of Islam was to be shown even in America, where, by the

One of the most curious aspects of the pilgrimage, at least to the non-Muslim, is the "running," which is thought to draw its inspiration from the banished biblical handmaiden Hagar's frantic search for water to nurture her infant son sired by Abraham. (According to this legend, it was the Angel Gabriel who uncovered the sacred well, Zemzem, enabling Hagar and her child to slake their thirst.) The obscure origins of this rite mean little to most hajjis, whose desire is precisely to replicate the Prophet's Last Pilgrimage, not to question his motivation. In Muhammad's day the hillocks of Safa and Marwa, symbolizing patience and perseverance, were exposed to the elements. Today they are fully enclosed, and pilgrims make the seven traditional circuits down mosaic-tiled corridors. As this view indicates, the ailing and disabled are wheeled in chairs down the center aisle of the place of running.

middle of the twentieth century, a dominant school of art was based on abstraction. Here is not the place to inquire deeply into the reasons that prompted Westerners to break, at least temporarily, with a tradition of representative art that could trace its way back through Victorian and Bourbon paintings to the Renaissance, which in turn looked back to Greece and Rome. In part, though, it may have been prompted by such negative factors as the devaluing of a civilization that had so recently shown itself impotent against great wars and monumental crimes. On another level, too, an economy based on computers was necessarily nearer in spirit to abstract symbols than to copies of human bodies in marble or bronze. In a more positive sense, Western artists undoubtedly saw the oneness of the planet, a oneness effected by a revolution in transportation and communication. All human actions, good and bad, met on the television screen, enabling viewers to see, as never before, how human societies are interconnected.

In its openness to new ideas the twentieth century offers parallels to the seventh, when Islam burst from Arabia to vanquish, by force of appeal as well as arms, such fatigued empires as Byzantium and Persia. While comparatively few Westerners actually embraced modern Islam, many more were prepared to be influenced in their attitudes by the Koran, the Sufi mystical movement, or Islamic art. Participants in a popular survey conducted in America in the late 1970s chose, from a list of a hundred famous men that included Newton and Jesus, the Prophet Muhammad as the individual who had most deeply affected the course of history.

Speculating on what might have happened if Islam had not been defeated in France in 732 by Charles

The muezzins' last call floats out over rose-red Mecca at dusk, and all Muslims within earshot cease their labors and prostrate themselves in the direction of the Sacred Mosque. They are joined, in that moment, by uncounted millions around the globe, all responding to a call they may hear only in some inner ear—and all replying, in unison, with the ancient, alliterative phrase: "Labbaika allahumma labbaika—I am here, God, at your command!"

Martel, the eighteenth-century historian Edward Gibbon wrote:

> A victorious line of march had been prolonged above a thousand miles from the rock of Gibraltar to the banks of the Loire; the repetition of an equal space would have carried the Saracens to the confines of Poland and the Highlands of Scotland: the Rhine is not more impassable than the Nile or the Euphrates, and the Arabian fleet might have sailed without a naval combat into the mouth of the Thames. Perhaps the interpretation of the Koran would now be taught in the schools of Oxford, and her pulpits might demonstrate to a circumcised people the sanctity and truth of the revelation of Mahomet [Muhammad].

Islam made no such conquest of course, but the Koran is taught today in the schools of Oxford—and in Mecca the sight of a Western face or the sound of idiomatic American, whether from Harlem or academe, is no longer particularly remarked. The world in general looks on the Kaaba and the great international concourse it inspires each year with increased interest and respect. And the fact that Mecca extends its welcome only to the faithful is more easily understood in a world overrun by tourists on the move.

While these shifts in attitude affect the way the world looks at Mecca, the city itself has been overwhelmed by change from another direction. That change began in December 1924, when Abdul Aziz ibn Saud, who had united most of the peninsula with the help of his *Ikhwan*, entered Mecca determined to enforce the ideals of Wahhabism on the city of the Prophet. The reformation

he envisioned involved both religious and moral issues, and under ibn Saud's aegis many superstitious practices were ended: guides were no longer permitted to conduct the faithful to miscellaneous shrines and defraud them of their cash; alcohol, which had been clandestinely available, fell under total prohibition; and the application of strict Islamic law made Mecca a city where a purse of gold left lying in the street was not touched, let alone stolen. Prostitution was forbidden, along with mixed bathing, Western dancing, and the appearance in public of unveiled women. Such measures did much to stiffen Islamic morale, but the development of the kingdom's medical and educational services lagged far behind, crippled by a shortage of funds. The Saudi Arabia of the 1920s was true to its principles, but poor—so poor that the proud Saudis were obliged to accept a British subsidy of £100,000 a year simply because it was so sorely needed.

All this was to change with the receipt of royalties derived from the discovery of subterranean wealth. In 1933 the United States secured the first concession to prospect for oil in the peninsula, and to exploit that oil if found. The Saudi decision to opt for American assistance in the development of the country's resources made sense at that time, in part because the other nations involved in the extraction and marketing of petroleum—chiefly Britain, France, and Holland—were still heavily involved in administering Arab and other Muslim colonies. Britain had lost much of its wartime popularity with the Arabs by applying the Balfour Declaration, whose threatened end result was the dispossession of Palestinians in favor of Jews. French attempts to integrate Algeria into metropolitan France

Muslims may visit Ise, the most sacred of Japan's Shinto shrines. And Muslims may tour St. Peter's, the first see of Christendom. But non-Muslims may not, under any circumstances, set foot in Mecca. The holy city of Islam was declared off-limits to non-believers when Muhammad seized power in A.D. 630, and that prohibition is strictly enforced to this day by the Saudi dynasty that now administers the Sacred Mosque and its precincts. It is, in fact, the very preservation of Mecca as hallowed ground, never to be knowingly defiled by non-Muslims, that gives the city its special appeal, not its religious art and architecture.

were equally resented. America, which at that time lacked even a rudimentary intelligence agency, was still identified with the ideals of President Wilson. Moreover, American skills in petroleum technology were known to the Saudis.

In 1938, five years after the first oil concession was awarded and on the eve of World War II, oil was discovered at Dhahran. At that time the wage-rate for Saudi employees was twelve cents a day. The needs of war, and then an affluence consequent on the postwar recovery of Germany and Japan, led to a rapid spiraling of oil production and oil receipts. At first, the new revenues were often seen as windfalls, and squandered. But with the accession of King Feisal, who succeeded his deposed brother ibn Saud in 1958, a high proportion of the oil revenues was devoted to internal development. These revenues were to be vastly increased after the October War of 1973 against Israel, when a temporary boycott led to a continuing increase in the price of the world's most sought-after fuel.

Saudi Arabia's transformation into one of the richest countries in the world was to affect Mecca directly. It coincided with similar, if less spectacular, developments in many other Islamic countries. During the 1970s Nigeria, Algeria, Libya, Iraq, the Gulf Emirates, and Iran were all to experience sudden oil-engendered increases in national revenue, and thus the title *hajji* suddenly became accessible to the multitudes who could afford a ticket to Mecca. Instead of the two years set aside by the medieval pilgrim ibn Jubayr, or the seven years it often took an African laborer of the nineteenth century to work his way to Mecca, a single week was sufficient for the mechanic from Algiers, the physician from Kara-

chi, and the merchant from Nairobi to fulfill their duties. It was comparatively easy for them to bring their wives. The brevity of the modern *hajj* also made it possible for rulers, normally reluctant to leave an unguarded chair, to visit Mecca and exchange ideas with fellow Muslims.

This proliferation of pilgrims dictated changes in Mecca that the new revenues of Saudi Arabia, as Guardian of the Holy Places, have made feasible. The need to expand the free space around the Kaaba has been a recurrent one since Omar first bought—and then pulled down—the houses surrounding the seventh-century shrine to afford space for circumambulation and reverent prayer. But from medieval times until the Saudi conquest of Mecca in 1924, the area inside the colonnades of the Sacred Mosque contained other buildings besides the Kaaba. The largest of these was the structure housing the Zemzem fountain, which Burckhardt described as "of a square shape, and of a massive construction."

Islam has four orthodox schools, which differ in small matters of interpretation and emphasis: the Hanafi, Maliki, Hanbali, and Shafi'i. In former times each had a separate place for prayer. The largest, the Makam (or "station of") Hanafi, was on the side of the Kaaba where rainwater from the roof (which is a few inches lower than the surrounding parapet) could pour through a golden spout of intricate device. The Makam Maliki, a third the size of its Hanafi counterpart, was situated on the west side of the Kaaba, while the Makam Hanbali stood not far from the Black Stone at the southeast corner. Burckhardt ascribed the upper story of the Zemzem building to the Shafi'i school, though

Burton argued that only the muezzin called there, the Shafi'ites traditionally prostrating themselves behind their imam, or religious leader, between the corner of the Zemzem building and the Makam Ibrahim.

This tradition of occupancy was ultimately to consume as much space as an entire building would have. In fact, there were two domed buildings for storing water jars, lamps, mats, brooms, and other impedimenta for the service of the mosque. And there was a lofty pulpit, used for the Friday sermon, and a wheeled staircase, used for approaching the raised door of the Kaaba. The Makam Ibrahim housed the stone on which Ibrahim had supposedly stood himself when rebuilding the Kaaba. A structure roughly six yards long by three broad, it was supported by six pillars, each roughly two and a half yards in height.

These buildings had few pretensions to architectural merit, nor were any of them of outstanding antiquity. They did, however, relieve the bare space of the large precinct, otherwise broken only by slightly raised causeways leading like fan blades toward the Kaaba. When the pilgrims numbered less than a hundred thousand, they experienced little inconvenience in circumambulating the Kaaba or prostrating themselves in prayer toward it. But new conditions of affluence and influx posed new problems for the guardians of the shrine. As one example, the Islamic World Association suggested to the late King Feisal in 1965—Year 1384 after the Migration—that the Station of Ibrahim be reduced in size by having the boulder set inside a protected case standing on a marble base, through whose grilles the pilgrims could see the relic. As executed, this new station somewhat recalls a sacred telephone kiosk without an

Curiously, the most potent emblem of Islam is almost without significance to Muslims themselves. The Black Stone, which may be a meteorite fragment and probably came originally from Iraq, is all but universally recognized as the prepotent symbol of Islam—which explains why it was carried off like some royal hostage by the Iraqis who beseiged Mecca in the tenth century. Damaged in that campaign, it nestles today within a silver boss set into the southeast corner of the Kaaba. Muslims attribute no special properties to the Black Stone, saluting it only because the Prophet did so on his final pilgrimage. In doing so they repeat Caliph Omar's declaration, directed to the Stone shortly after Muhammad's death: "I know well that you are a stone which can do neither good nor evil, and unless I had seen the Prophet, on whom be prayer and the blessings of God, kiss·you, I would not kiss you."

The arrival of the Age of Oil altered Mecca as it altered every city in Arabia. Overnight wealth led to overnight growth, and incalculable income resulted in ill-calculated construction. As these buildings went up, old ones came down—and they brought down with them much that was identifiably Islamic about the architecture of the Island of the Arabs. More than merely undistinguished, many of these structures were poorly adapted to Mecca's arid climate, against which the thick masonry walls and the wooden shutters (left) of an earlier era afford far better protection.

easily opening door. The protective structure contains 3,740 pounds of copper, and even so takes up so much less room than the building it replaces that an additional width of five yards has been secured for circumambulation by the faithful.

A second decision made under Feisal was to remove the entire superstructure of the Zemzem; access to the sacred waters is now down a sloping marble stairway. This too has freed up the sacred precinct around the Kaaba, although not so much as would a proposed project, which would involve the bodily removal of everything to do with the hallowed fountain, its water being piped underground to taps in some convenient edifice outside the precinct.

During the first years of affluence it was also decided to greatly enlarge the Sacred Mosque. At first royal architects discussed dismantling the entire outer frame of the Ottoman mosque, whose colonnades contained, according to Burckhardt's estimate, 554 pillars and whose roof was topped by 118 domes. The East often welcomes such radical innovations, provided they are sufficiently lavish. The passion to preserve the old, which in countries such as Britain has produced a conservationist movement typified by the twentieth-century poet John Betjeman, is still uncommon in the Middle East. Yet in the case of the Sacred Mosque a moderate victory was won for conservation: instead of pulling down the old mosque, Saudi architects contrived to encapsulate it inside a vast new shrine. This structure's colonnades were on two levels, and they were surmounted by a huge flat roof that could be used for prayer. A narrow space, like the air pocket between panes in double glazing, divided the skin of the old mosque from the colonnades of the new. When completed, the new Saudi mosque covered an area of 160,618 square yards, more than five times the size of the enclosed original. Instead of the nineteen gates Burckhardt listed, there were now sixty-four of varying sizes.

A second area to be transformed and then incorporated into the Saudi mosque was the sacred course, or *Mas'aa*. In the nineteenth century, as in the ninth, the course had been run—at a slow trot by men, at a walking pace by women—along a busy thoroughfare. There was poetry in this juxtaposition of the observance of an ancient rite with the everyday life of a bazaar, and also confusion. The runner had his thoughts on eternity, or at least fixed on the past, while the road bustled with sellers of lemonade and prayer beads. But what was a tolerable and picturesque muddle in the nineteenth century became an impossibility in the age of oil. To alleviate the resultant confusion, the place of running was entirely enclosed. Access to the new *Mas'sa* is now conveniently secured from inside the mosque, and if one were to invoke a commercial comparison today, it would no longer be with a bazaar, since the new structure is air-conditioned, ornate, and spacious, but with the sort of mall a modern department store might construct to link its home-furnishings basement with the nearby subway. This mall is in two tiers, each eight thousand square yards in extent and each subdivided down the middle for two-way traffic.

Seen from a helicopter, the new mosque differs in shape from the approximate rectangle, 250 paces long by 200 broad, that the Ottomans knew. It now resembles a mammoth latchkey, with the colonnaded precinct as the head and the sacred course as the shaft. The new

A Western journalist, doubtless caught up in the hyperbolic excess that characterized the event, described the 1969 Woodstock Music Festival as "the largest peaceable gathering in human history." That writer was wrong, of course. In that year—and in every year thereafter—the largest peaceable assembly of humanity in all history recurred in Mecca. In the season of the pilgrimage many times the number who gathered at Woodstock converge on Mecca from all corners of the compass, intent upon rededicating themselves to Allah.

mosque is so capacious that five hundred thousand worshipers may pray at one time, and should more space be needed, the main doors give onto five great squares that have been gouged from the town adjacent to the mosque.

Conical Mount Arafat, not the Kaaba, is the hub of the pilgrimage. In former times pilgrims deemed it meritorious to walk the five miles from Mecca east to Arafat; others moved to the sacred mount on camel- or horseback. Now air-conditioned cars speed *ihram*-clad figures to Arafat on a superhighway, little different from those in Europe or America. The age of oil, it might be said, has both inspired and paid for these transformations. The once-straggling village of Muna, for instance, now resembles a concrete flyover.

No innovation has been made without a reason, yet few changes have improved the aesthetics of Islam's chief shrine. Whether the ancient door into the Kaaba will be more beautiful when it is refurbished—a current Saudi undertaking, and by all reports a colossally costly one—will be for the faithful to decide. Most Westerners will be unable to judge, except from photographs, for the Saudis continue to enforce the ban on non-Muslims entering Mecca, just as they have the legal sanctions enjoined by the Koran. In this bustling city of cars and gasoline fumes it is still the custom, for example, for murderers to be killed in public.

Most Arabs, tired of being mere figures in a picturesque landscape, welcome modernity when it reaches them in the shape of large cars and plush hotels. Younger architects, however, are beginning to proclaim merit in ancient modes. Narrow lanes, window grilles, and covered markets, they note, suit a burning climate better than open piazzas and wide streets. Mohammad Jamil Brownson, an Islamic writer whose last name suggests Western origin, has stressed that modern architectural horrors can too easily replace the old. "The 'barren valley' of which Allah speaks to us in the Koran has been artificially transformed into an urban metropolis by a completely alien, imported technology," Brownson writes. "The city is rapidly being redesigned to serve the automobile rather than human beings." Identifying the "notorious automobile" as the culprit, Brownson somewhat wistfully proposes that if everyone—with the exception of the old and the handicapped—were to walk into Mecca, "the entire 'traffic problem' would evaporate."

Ziauddin Sardar, another specialist on the *hajj*, stresses the damage modern technology has done to the spiritual nature of the pilgrimage: "The dominant theme during the Hajj is the assimilation of the pilgrim with the will of God. This assimilation results, in part, from prayer, inner reflection and meditation. The major requirement for prayer and reflection is peace: peace within and peace without, peace with Allah and peace with one's soul, peace with one another and peace with the environment, peace with birds, animals and even with insects." Like Brownson, Sardar attacks the car as a violator of this state of peace. "It is difficult, nay quite impossible, to be in a constant state of peace amidst the automotive nightmare," he notes, railing against "the perpetual noise of motor vehicles, helicopters and aeroplanes; the ear-piercing shrieks of horns and sirens; the continuous chants of competing loudspeakers; the horrific music of the transistors and the pungent smell and suffocating exhaust fumes."

In ancient times the color of the kiswa covering the Kaaba varied with the color of the reigning Caliph's banner. Now it is always black, and the business of creating each year's covering provides full-time employ for more than one hundred artisans. These weavers (left, below) and embroiderers (below) are descended from the family guilds charged with renewing the kiswa generation after generation. The product of their labors contains 2,500 square feet of cloth and weighs two tons, considerably more than the earliest kiswas, which were made in Egypt and brought by caravan, a journey that often took forty days. A portion of the total weight is pure gold, used to embroider both the frieze that circles the top of the Kaaba and the so-called veil (left, above), which drapes over the cube-like structure's single door.

Arabs refer to it as "the days of drying out"—the sacrifice of nearly a million camels (right, above) and goats (right, below) that marks the climax of the hajj. But a Westerner who visited Mecca in the nineteenth century had another name for it: "This Devil's Punchbowl" was his appellation for the vast abattoir at Muna, outside Mecca, where home-bound hajjis dried the carcasses of recently slaughtered animals in order to make up rations for their long journey home.

OVERLEAF: Seen from the air, the Sacred Mosque looks rather like a mammoth latchkey: the Kaaba and its surrounding colonnades form the head, and the place of running, once open-air and now fully enclosed, forms the shaft. Seen during the off season, sun-baked and serene, the holy heart of Islam seems somewhat isolated from the rest of Mecca. But come the hajj, *those open areas fill with the faithful, bent on undeviating repetition of rites set down fifteen centuries ago.*

Significantly, these criticisms have been published under the auspices of the Hajj Research Centre of Jiddah, the port of entry for most pilgrims. The center may be able to plan action to meet Sardar's complaints, and he, for one, is convinced that it should. "Walking on the pathways used by the Prophet," he writes, "can be phenomenally uplifting. Driving through formidable traffic jams, or plodding on concrete roads, dodging cars and human waste and debris generates only fatigue. In present-day Muna what is experienced is not the environment of the Prophet, but the surroundings of Manhattan." And, Sardar adds, "many pilgrims spend much of their time during Hajj avoiding filth and debris rather than in prayer and supplication."

On no soul, the Koran proclaims, does God place a burden greater than it can bear. There is no reason to suppose that this is not true also of cities, which are collections of souls. The existence of the Hajj Research Centre and its publications prove that the concerned imagination exists, and the merest glance at the estimated royalties of the Saudi kingdom shows that the power to translate proposal into answer exists as well. It is probably safe to predict that the anonymous African whom Burckhardt saw in 1814, prostrating himself toward the lamplit Kaaba, will be followed by men and women from every continent, seeking a foretaste of Paradise or spiritual peace. Unless there intervenes that apocalyptic "carding of the hills" that the Koran predicts, the House that was ancient when Muhammad was young will remain a vivid focus when a hundred generations have passed to their reward.

MECCA IN LITERATURE

"Our notions of Mecca must be drawn from the Arabians; as no unbeliever is permitted to enter the city, our travellers are silent," wrote the great English historian Edward Gibbon in the late eighteenth century—and at the time his monumental, multivolume Decline and Fall of the Roman Empire *was published, Gibbon was entirely correct. A mere half century later, however, European unbelievers would succeed in reaching forbidden Mecca, and their reports would flesh out the bare-bones description of the "Caaba" that Gibbon offers in his opus magnus.*

The genuine antiquity (of) the Caaba ascends beyond the Christian era: in describing the coast of the Red Sea the Greek historian Diodorus has remarked, between the Thamudites and the Sabeans, a famous temple, whose superior sanctity was revered by *all* the Arabians; the linen or silken veil, which is annually renewed by the Turkish emperor, was first offered by a pious king of the Homerites, who reigned seven hundred years before the time of Mohammed. A tent or a cavern might suffice for the worship of the savages, but an edifice of stone and clay has been erected in its place; and the art and power of the monarchs of the East have been confined to the simplicity of the original model. A spacious portico encloses the quadrangle of the Caaba—a square chapel twenty-four cubits long, twenty-three broad, and twenty-seven high: a door and a window admit the light; the double roof is supported by three pillars of wood; a spout (now of gold) discharges the rain-water, and the well Zemzem is protected by a dome from accidental pollution. The tribe of Koreish, by fraud or force, had acquired the custody of the Caaba: the sacerdotal office devolved through four lineal descents to the grandfather of Mohammed; and the family of the Hashemites, from whence he sprung, was the most respectable and sacred in the eyes of their country. The precincts of Mecca enjoyed the rights of sanctuary; and in the last month of each year the city and the temple were crowded with a long train of pilgrims, who presented their vows and offerings in the house of God. The same rites which are now accomplished by the faithful Musulman were invented and practised by the superstition of the idolatera. At an awful distance they cast away their garments: seven times with hasty steps they encircled the Caaba, and kissed the black stone: seven times they visited and adored the adjacent mountains: seven times they threw stones into the valley of Mina: and the pilgrimage was achieved, as at the present hour, by a sacrifice of sheep and camels, and the burial of their hair and nails in the consecrated ground. Each tribe either found or introduced in the Caaba their domestic worship: the temple was adorned, or defiled, with three hundred and sixty idols of men, eagles, lions, and antelopes; and most conspicuous was the statue of Hebal, of red agate, holding in his hand seven arrows without heads or feathers, the instruments and symbols of profane divination. But this statue was a monument of Syrian arts: the devotion of the ruder ages was content with a pillar or a tablet; and the rocks of the desert were hewn into gods or altars in imitation of the black stone of Mecca, which is deeply tainted with the reproach of an idolatrous origin. From Japan to Peru the use of sacrifice has universally prevailed; and the votary has expressed his gratitude or fear by destroying or consuming, in honour of the gods, the dearest and most precious of their gifts. The life of a man is the most precious oblation to deprecate a public calamity: the altars of Phoenicia and Egypt, of Rome and Carthage, have been polluted with human gore: the cruel practice was long preserved among the Arabs; in the third century a boy was annually sacrificed by the tribe of the Dumatians; and a royal captive was piously slaughtered by the prince of the

Saracens, the ally and soldier of the emperor Justinian. A parent who drags his son to the altar exhibits the most painful and sublime effort of fanatacism: the deed or the intention was sanctified by the example of saints and heroes; and the father of Mohammed himself was devoted by a rash vow, and hardly ransomed for the equivalent of a hundred camels. In the time of ignorance the Arabs, like the Jews and Egyptians, abstained from the taste of swine's flesh; they circumcised their children at the age of puberty: the same customs, without the censure or the precept of the Koran, have been silently transmitted to their posterity and proselytes. It has been sagaciously conjectured that the artful legislator indulged the stubborn prejudices of his countrymen. It is more simple to believe that he adhered to the habits and opinions of his youth, without foreseeing that a practice congenial to the climate of Mecca might become useless or inconvenient on the banks of the Danube or the Volga.

EDWARD GIBBON
*History of the Decline and Fall
of the Roman Empire, 1776–88*

"FOR THIS IS PARADISE!"

One of the significant side-effects of Napoleon Bonaparte's Egyptian expedition of 1798 was a rekindling of Western interest in all of the Middle East—including the Hijaz. And in the first decades of the new century Europeans in increasing numbers were to gain entrance to Islam's holiest city. They came in mufti, disguised as pilgrims from Muslim nations; and perhaps because Mecca is a city perpetually jammed with religious tourists from every corner of the globe, their masquerades went undetected. And thus it was, in the early 1800s, that a Swiss adventurer named John Lewis Burckhardt was able to enter Mecca and file these impressions.

Where the valley is wider than in other interior parts of the town, stands the mosque, called Beitullah, or El Haram, a building remarkable only on account of the Kaaba, which it encloses; for there are several mosques in other places of the East nearly equal to this in size, and much superior to it in beauty.

The Kaaba stands in an oblong square, two hundred and fifty paces long, and two hundred broad, none of the sides of which run quite in a straight line, though at first sight the whole appears to be of a regular shape. This open square is enclosed on the eastern side by a colonnade: the pillars stand in a quadruple row: they are three deep on the other sides, and united by pointed arches, every four of which support a small dome, plastered and whitened on the outside. These domes, according to Kotobeddyn, are one hundred and fifty-two in number. Along the whole colonnade, on the four sides, lamps are suspended from the arches. Some are lighted every night, and all during the nights of Ramadhan. The pillars are above twenty feet in height, and generally from one foot and a half to one foot and three quarters in diameter; but little regularity has been observed in regard to them. Some are of white marble, granite, or porphyry, but the greater number are of common stone of the Mekka mountains. El Fasy states the whole at five hundred and eighty-nine, and says they are all of marble, excepting one hundred and twenty-six, which are of common stone, and three of composition. Kotobeddyn reckons five hundred and fifty-five, of which, according to him, three hundred and eleven are of marble, and the rest of stone taken from the neighboring mountains; but neither of these authors lived to see the latest repairs of the mosque, after the destruction occasioned by a torrent, in A.D. 1626. Between every three or four columns stands an octagonal one, about four feet in thickness. On the east side are two shafts of reddish gray granite, in one piece, and one fine gray porphyry column with slabs of white feldspath. On the north side is one red granite column, and one of five-grained red prophyry: these are probably the columns which Kotobeddyn states to have been brought from Egypt, and principally from Akhmim (Panopolis), when the chief El Mohdy enlarged the mosque, in A.H. 163. Among the four hundred and fifty or five hundred columns, which form the enclosure, I found not any two capitals or bases exactly alike: the capitals are of coarse Saracen workmanship; some of them, which had served for former buildings, by the ignorance of the workmen have been placed upside down upon the shafts. I observed about half a dozen marble bases of good Grecian workmanship. A few of the marble columns bear Arabic or Cufic inscriptions, in which I read the dates 863 and 762. (A.H.). A column on the east side exhibits a very ancient Cufic inscription, somewhat defaced, which I could neither read nor copy. Those shafts, formed of the Mekka stone, cut principally from the side of the mountain near the Shebeyka quarter, are mostly in three pieces, but the marble shafts are in one piece. Some of the columns are strengthened with broad iron rings or bands, as in many other Saracen buildings of the East: they were first employed here by Ibn Dhaher Berkouk, King of Egypt, in rebuilding the mosque, which had been destroyed by fire in A.H. 802.

This temple has been so often ruined and repaired, that no traces of remote antiquity are to be found about it. On the inside of the great wall which encloses the colonnades, a single Arabic inscription is seen, in large characters, but containing merely the names of Mohammed and his immediate successors: Abou Beker, Omar, Othman, and Aly. The name of Allah, in large characters, occurs also in several places. On the outside, over the gates, are long inscriptions, in the Solouth character, commemorating the names of those by whom the gates were built, long and minute details of which are given by the historians of Mekka. The inscription on the south side, over Bab Ibrahim, is most conspicuous; all that side was rebuilt by the Egyptian Sultan El Ghoury, in A.H. 906. Over the Bab Aly and Bab Abbas is a long inscription, also in the Solouth character, placed there by Sultan Murad Ibn Soleyman, in A.H. 984, after he had repaired the whole building. Kotobeddyn has given this inscription at length; it occupies several pages in his history, and is a monument of the Sultan's vanity. This side of the mosque having escaped destruction in 1626, the inscription remains uninjured.

Some parts of the walls and arches are gaudily painted, in stripes of yellow, red, and blue, as are also the minarets. Paintings of flowers, in the usual Muselman style, are no where seen; the floors of the colonnades are paved with large stones badly cemented together.

Seven paved causeways lead from the colonnades towards the Kaaba, or holy house, in the center. They are of sufficient breadth to admit four or five persons to walk abreast, and they are elevated about nine inches above the ground. Between these causeways, which are covered with fine gravel or sand, grass appears growing in several places, produced by the Zemzem water dozing out of the jars, which are placed in the ground in long rows during the day. The whole area of the mosque is upon a lower level than any of the streets surrounding it. There is a descent of eight or ten steps from the gates on the north side into the platform of the colonnade, and of three or four steps from the gates, on the south side.

Towards the middle of this area stands the Kaaba; it is one hundred and fifteen paces from the north colonnade, and eighty-eight from the south. For this want of symmetry we may readily account, the Kaaba having existed prior to the mosque, which was built around it, and enlarged at different periods. The Kaaba is an oblong massive structure, eighteen paces in length, fourteen in breadth, and from thirty-five to forty feet in height. I took the bearing of one of its longest sides, and found it to be N.N.W.½W. It is constructed of the grey Mekka stone, in large blocks of different sizes, joined together in a very rough manner, and with bad cement. It was entirely rebuilt as it now stands in A.D. 1627: the torrent, in the preceding year, had thrown down three of its sides; and preparatory to its re-erection, the fourth side was, according to Asamy, pulled down, after the olemas, or learned divines, had been consulted on the question, whether mortals might be permitted to destroy any part of the holy edifice without incurring the charge of sacrilege and infidelity.

The Kaaba stands upon a base two feet in height, which presents a sharp inclined plane; its roof being flat, it has at a distance the appearance of a perfect cube. The only door which affords entrance, and which is opened but two or three times in the year, is on the north side, and about seven feet above the ground. In entering it, therefore, wooden steps are used—of them I shall speak hereafter. In the first periods of Islam, however, when it was rebuilt in A.H. 64, by Ibn Zebeyr, chief of Mekka, the nephew of Aysha, it had two doors even with the ground-floor of the mosque. The present door (which, according to Azraky, was brought hither from Constantinople in 1633), is wholly coated with silver, and has several gilt ornaments. Upon its threshold are placed every night various small lighted wax candles, and perfuming-pans, filled with musk, aloe-wood, &c.

At the northeast corner of the Kaaba, near the door, is the famous "Black Stone"; it forms a part of the sharp angle of the building, at four or five feet above the ground. It is an irregular oval, about seven inches in diameter, with an undulated surface, composed of about a dozen smaller stones of different sizes and shapes, well joined together with a small quantity of cement, and perfectly smoothed: it looks as if the whole had been broken into many pieces by a violent blow, and then united again. It is very difficult to determine accurately the quality of this stone, which has been worn to its present surface by the millions of touches and kisses it has received. It appeared to me like a lava, containing several small extraneous particles, of a whitish and of a yellowish substance. Its color is now a deep reddish brown, approaching to black: it is surrounded on all sides by a border, composed of a substance which I took to be a close cement of pitch and gravel, of a similar, but not quite the same brownish color. This border serves to support its detached pieces; it is two or three inches in breadth, and rises a little above the surface of the stone. Both the border and the stone itself are encircled by a silver band, broader below than above and on the two sides, with a considerable swelling below, as if a part of the stone were hidden under it. The lower part of the border is studded with silver nails.

In the southeast corner of the Kaaba, or, as the Arabs call it, Roken el Yemány, there is another stone, about five feet from the ground; it is one foot and a half in length, and two inches in breadth, placed upright, and of the common Mekka stone. This the people walking round the Kaaba touch only with the right hand: they do not kiss it.

On the north side of the Kaaba, just by its door, and close to the wall, is a slight yellow hollow in the ground, lined with marble, and sufficiently large to admit of three persons sitting. Here it is thought meritorious to pray: the spot is called El Madjen, and supposed to be that where Abraham and his son Ismayl kneaded the chalk and mud which they used in building the Kaaba; and near this Madjen, the former is said to have placed the large stone upon which he stood while working at the masonry. On the basis of the Kaaba, just over the Madjen, is an ancient Cufic inscription; but this I was unable to decipher, and had no opportunity of copying it. I do not find it mentioned by any of the historians.

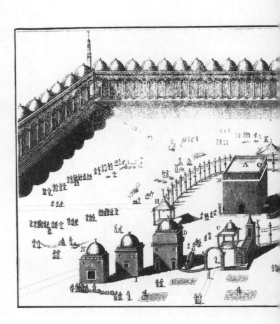

On the west side of the Kaaba, about two feet below its summit, is the famous Myzab, or water-spout, through which the rainwater collected on the roof of the building is discharged, so as to fall upon the ground; it is about four feet in length, and six inches in breadth, as well as I could judge from below, with borders equal in height to its breadth. At the mouth, hangs what is called the beard of the Myzab, a gilt board, over which the water falls. This spout was sent hither from Constantinople in A.H. 981, and is *reported* to be of pure gold. The pavement round the Kaaba, below the Myzab, was laid down in A.H. 826, and consists of various colored stones, forming a very handsome specimen of mosaic. There are two large slabs of fine *verde-antico* in the center, which, according to Makrizi, were sent thither as presents from Cairo, in A.H. 241. This is the spot where, according to Mohammedan tradition, Ismayl, the son of Ibrahim, or Abraham, and his mother Hagar, are buried; and here it is meritorious for the pilgrim to recite a prayer of two rikats. On this west side is a semicircular wall, the two extremities of which are in a line with the sides of the Kaaba, and distant from it three or four feet, leaving an opening which leads to the burying-place of Ismayl. The wall bears the name of El Hatym, and the area which it encloses is called Hedjer, or Hedjer Ismayl, on account of its being separated from the Kaaba: the wall itself, also, is something so called; and the name Hatym is given by the historians to the space of ground between the Kaaba and the wall on one side, and the Bir Zemzem and Makam Ibrahim on the other. The present Mekkawys, however, apply the name Hatym to the wall only.

Tradition says that the Kaaba once extended as far as the Hatym, and that this side having fallen down just at the time of the Hadj, the expenses of repairing it were demanded from the pilgrims, under a pretence that the revenues of government were not acquired in a manner sufficiently pure to admit of their application toward a purpose so sacred, whilst the money of the hadjys would possess the requisite sanctity. The sum, however, obtained from them, proved very inadequate: all that could be done, therefore, was to raise a wall, which marked the space formerly occupied by the Kaaba. This tradition, although current among the Metowefs, is at variance with history, which declares that the Hedjer was built by the Beni Koreysh, who contracted the dimensions of the Kaaba; that it was united to the building by Hadjadj, and again separated from it by Ibn Zebeyr. It is asserted by Fasy, that a part of the Hedjer, as it now stands, was never comprehended within the Kaaba. The law regards it as a portion of the Kaaba, inasmuch as it is esteemed equally meritorious to pray in the Hedjer as in the Kaaba itself; and the pilgrims who have not an opportunity of entering the latter, are permitted to affirm upon oath that they have prayed in the Kaaba, although they may have only prostrated themselves within the enclosure of the Hatym. The wall is

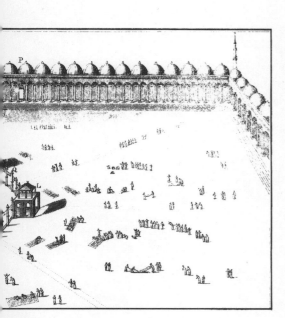

built of solid stone, about five feet in height, and four in thickness, cased all over with white marble, and inscribed with prayers and invocations, neatly sculptured upon the stone in modern characters. These and the casing are the work of El Ghoury, the Egyptian Sultan, in A.H. 917, as we learn from Kotobeddyn. The walk round the Kaaba is performed on the outside of the wall—the nearer to it the better.

The four sides of the Kaaba are covered with a black silk stuff, hanging down, and leaving the roof bare. This curtain, or veil, is called *kesoua*, and renewed annually at the time of the Hadj, being brought from Cairo, where it is manufactured at the Grand Seignoir's expense. On it are various prayers interwoven in the same color as the stuff, and it is, therefore extremely difficult to read them. A little above the middle, and running round the whole building, is a line of similar inscriptions, worked in gold thread. That part of the kesoua which covers the door is richly embroidered with silver. Openings are left for the Black Stone, and the other in the southeast corner, which thus remain uncovered. The kesoua is always of the same form and pattern; that which I saw on my first visit to the mosque, was in a decayed state, and full of holes. On the 25th of the month Zul' Kade the old one is taken away, and the Kaaba continues without a cover for fifteen days. It is then said that *El Kaaba Yehrem*, "The Kaaba has assumed the ihram," which lasts until the tenth of Zul Hadje, the day of the return of the pilgrims from Arafat to Wady Muna, when the new kesoua is put on. During the first days, the new covering is tucked up by cords fastened to the roof, so as to leave the lower part of the building exposed: having remained thus for some days, it is let down, and covers the whole structure, being then tied to strong brass rings in the basis of the Kaaba. The removal of the old kesoua was performed in a very indecorous manner; and a contest ensued among the hadjys and people of Mekka, both young and old, about a few rags of it. The hadjys even collect the dust which sticks to the walls of the Kaaba, under the kesoua, and sell it, on their return, as a sacred relic. At the moment the building is covered, and completely bare (*uryan*, as it is styled) a crowd of women assembled round it, rejoicing with cries called "Walwalou."

The black color of the kesoua, covering the large cube in the midst of a vast square, gives to the Kaaba, at first sight, a very singular and imposing appearance; as it is not fastened down tightly, the slightest breeze causes it to move in slow undulations, which are hailed with prayers by the congregation assembled around the building, as a sign of the presence of its guardian angels, whose wings, by their motion, are supposed to be the cause of the waving of the covering. Seventy thousand angels have the Kaaba in their holy care, and are ordered to transport it to Paradise, when the trumpet of the last judgment shall be sounded.

The clothing of the Kaaba was an ancient custom of the Pagan Arabs. The first kesoua, says El Azraky, was put on by Asad Toba, one of the Hamyarite kings of Yemen: before Islam it had two coverings, one for winter and the other for summer. In the early ages of Islam it was sometimes white and sometimes red, and consisted of the richest brocade. In subsequent times it was furnished by the different Sultans of Baghdad, Egypt, or Yemen, according to their respective influence over Mekka prevailed; for the clothing of the Kaaba appears to have always been considered as a proof of sovereignty over the Hedjaz. Kalaoun, Sultan of Egypt, assumed to himself and successors the exclusive right, and from them the Sultans at Constantinople have inherited it. Kalaoun appropriated the revenue of the two large villages Bysous and Sandabeir, in Lower Egypt, to the expense of the kesoua; and Sultan Solyman Ibn Selym subsequently added several others; but the Kaaba has long been deprived of this resource.

Round the Kaaba is a good pavement of marble, about eight inches below the level of the great square; it was laid in A.H. 981, by order of the Sultan, and describes an irregular oval; it is surrounded by thirty-two slender gilt pillars, or rather poles, between every two of which are suspended seven glass lamps, always lighted after sunset. Beyond the poles is a second pavement, about eight paces broad, somewhat elevated above the first, but of coarser work; then another, six inches higher, and eighteen paces broad, upon which stand several small buildings; beyond this is the gravelled ground, so that two broad steps may be said to lead from the square down to the Kaaba. . . .

The gravel-ground, and part of the adjoining outer pavement of the Kaaba, is covered, at the time of evening prayers, with carpets of from sixty to eighty feet in length, and four feet in breadth, of Egyptian manufacture, which are rolled up after prayers. The greater part of the hadjys bring their own carpets with them. The more distant parts of the area, and the floor under the colonnade, are spread with mats, brought from Souakin; the latter situation being the usual place for the performance of the midday and afternoon prayers. Many of these mats are presented to the mosque by the hadjys, for which they have in return the satisfaction of seeing their names inscribed on them in large characters.

At sunset, great numbers assemble for the first evening prayer: they form themselves into several wide circles, sometimes as many as twenty, around the Kaaba as a common center before which every person makes his prostration; and thus, as the Mohammedan doctors observe, Mekka is the only spot throughout the world in which the true believer can, with propriety, turn during his prayers toward any point of the compass. The Imám takes his post near the gate of the Kaaba, and his genuflexions are imitated by the whole assembled multitude. The effect of the joint prostrations of six or eight thousand persons, added to the recollection of the distance and various quarters from whence they come, and for what purpose, cannot fail to impress the most cool-minded spectator with some degree of awe. At night, when the lamps are lighted, and numbers of devotees are performing the Towaf round the Kaaba, the sight of the busy crowds—the voices of the Metowefs, intent upon making themselves heard by those to whom they recite their prayers— the loud conversation of many idle persons—the running, playing, and laughing of boys, give to the whole a very different appearance, and one more resembling that of a place of public amusement. The crowd, however, leaves the mosque about nine o'clock, when it again becomes the place of silent meditation and prayer, to the *few* visitors who are led to the spot by sincere piety, and not worldly motives or fashion.

There is an opinion prevalent at Mekka, founded on holy tradition, that the mosque will contain any number of the faithful; and that if even the whole Mohammedan community were to enter at once, they would all find room in it to pray. The guardian angels, it is said, would invisibly extend the dimensions of the building, and diminish the size of each individual. The fact is, that during the most numerous pilgrimages, the mosque, which can contain, I believe, about thirty-five thousand persons in the act of prayer, is never half filled. Even on Fridays, the greater part of the Mekkawys, contrary to the injunctions of the law, pray at home, if at all, and many hadjys follow their example. I could never count more than ten thousand individuals in the mosque at one time, even after the return from Arafat, when the whole body of hadjys were collected, for a few days, in and about the city. . . .

The termination of the Hadj gives a very different appearance to the temple. Disease and mortality, which succeed to the fatigues endured on the journey, or are caused by the light covering of the ihram, the unhealthy lodgings at Mekka, the bad fare, and sometimes absolute want, fill the mosque with dead bodies, carried thither to receive the Imám's prayer, or with sick persons, many of whom, when their dissolution approaches, are brought to the colonnades, that they may either be cured by a sight of the Kaaba, or at least have the satisfaction of expiring within the sacred enclosure. Poor hadjys, worn out with disease and hunger, are seen dragging their emaciated bodies along the columns; and when no longer able to stretch forth their hand to ask the passenger for charity, they place a bowl to receive alms near the mat on which they lay themselves. When they feel their last moments approaching, they cover themselves with their tattered garments; and often a whole day passes before it is discovered that they are dead. For a month subsequent to the conclusion of the Hadj, I found, almost every morning, corpses of pilgrims lying in the mosque; myself and a Greek hadjy, whom accident had brought to the spot, once closed the eyes of a poor Mogrebyn pilgrim, who had crawled into the neighborhood of the Kaaba, to breathe his last, as the Moslems say, "in the arms of the prophet and of the guardian angels." He intimated by signs his wish that we should sprinkle Zemzem water over him; and while we were doing so, he expired: half an hour afterwards he was buried. There are several persons in the service of the mosque employed to wash carefully the spot on which those who expire in the mosque have lain, and to bury all the poor and friendless strangers who die at Mekka.

JOHN LEWIS BURCKHARDT
Travels in Arabia, 1829

BLACK AS THE WINGS OF SOME SPIRIT

In introducing Sir Richard Burton's Pilgrimage to Al-Madinah and Meccah *to English readers, his editor noted, with perfect accuracy, that "few but literati are aware of the existence of Lodovico Bartema's naïve recital" of his visit to Mecca. Or, for that matter, of the "quaint narrative of Joseph Pitts or of the wild journal of Giovanni Finati"—all of them written centuries before Burton's time. Curiously absent from this recital was the name of John Lewis Burckhardt, whose description of Mecca had been published a mere twenty-five years earlier and was, in many respects, superior to Burton's. Few but literati were in a position to compare the two, however, and Burton's version soon established itself as the definitive nineteenth-century account of Mecca.*

There at last it lay, the bourn of my long and weary Pilgrimage, realising the plans and hopes of many and many a year. The mirage medium of Fancy invested the huge catafalque and its gloomy pall with peculiar charms. There were no giant fragments of hoar antiquity as in Egypt, no remains of graceful and harmonious beauty as in Greece and Italy, no barbarous gorgeousness as in the buildings of India; yet the view was strange, unique—and how few have looked upon the celebrated shrine! I may truly say that, of all the worshippers who clung weeping to the curtain, or who pressed their beating hearts to the stone, none felt for the moment a deeper emotion than did the Haji from the far-north. It was as if the poetical legends of the Arab spoke truth, and that the waving wings of angels, not the sweet breeze of morning, were agitating and swelling the black covering of the shrine. But, to confess humbling truth, theirs was the high feeling of religious enthusiasm, mine was the ecstasy of gratified pride.

Few Moslems contemplate for the first time the Ka'abah, without fear and awe: there is a popular jest against new comers, that they generally inquire the direction of prayer. This being the Kiblah, or fronting place, Moslems pray all around it; a circumstance which of course cannot take place in any spot of Al-Islam but the Harim. The boy Mohammed, therefore, left me for a few minutes to myself; but presently he warned me that it was time to begin. Advancing, we entered through the Bab Benu Shaybah, the "Gate of the Sons of the Shaybah" (old woman). There we raised our hands, repeated the Labbayk, the Takbir, and the Tahlil; after which we uttered certain supplications, and drew our hands down our faces. Then we proceeded to the Shafe'is' place of worship—the open pavement between the Makam Ibrahim and the well Zemzem—where we performed the usual two-bow prayer in honour of the Mosque. This was followed by a cup of holy water and a present to the Sakkas, or carriers, who for the consideration distributed, in my name, a large earthen vaseful to poor pilgrims.

The word Zemzem has a doubtful origin. Some derive it from the Zam Zam, or murmuring of its waters, others from Zam! Zam! (fill! fill! i.e. the bottle), Hagar's impatient exclamation when she saw the stream. Sale translates it stay! stay! and says that Hagar called out in the Egyptian language, to prevent her son wandering. The Hukama, or Rationalists of Al-Islam, who invariably connect their faith with the worship of Venus, especially, and the heavenly bodies generally, derive Zemzem from the Persian, and make it signify the "great luminary." Hence they say the Zemzem, as well as the Ka'abah, denoting the Cuthite or Ammonian worship of sun and fire, deserves man's reverence. So [a Persian poet] addresses these two buildings:—

"O Ka'abah, thou traveller of the heavens!"
"O Venus, thou fire of the world!"

Thus Wahid Mohammed, founder of the Wahidiyah sect, identifies the Kiblah and the sun; wherefore he says the door fronts the East. By the names Yaman ("right-hand"), Sham ("left-hand"), Kubul, or the East wind ("fronting"), and Dubur, or the West wind ("from the back"), it is evident that worshippers fronted the rising sun. According to the Hukama, the original Black Stone represents Venus, "which in the border of the heavens is a star of the planets," and symbolical of the generative power of nature, "by whose passive energy the universe was warmed into life and motion." The Hindus accuse the Moslems of adoring the Bayt Ullah.

"O Moslem, if thou worship the Ka'abah,
Why reproach the worshippers of idols?"

says Rai Manshar. And Musaylimah, who in his attempt to found a fresh faith, gained but the historic epithet of "Liar," allowed his followers to turn their faces in any direction, mentally ejaculating, "I address myself to thee, who hast neither side nor figure;" a doctrine which might be sensible in the abstract, but certainly not material enough and pride-flattering to win him many converts in Arabia. . . .

We then advanced towards the eastern angle of the Ka'abah, in which is inserted the Black Stone; and, standing about ten yards from it, repeated with upraised hands, "There is no god but Allah alone, Whose Covenant is Truth, and Whose Servant is Victorious. There is no god but Allah, without Sharer; His is the Kingdom, to Him be Praise, and He over all Things is potent." After which we approached as close as we could to the stone. A crowd of pilgrims preventing our touching it that time, we raised our hands to our ears, in the first position of prayer, and then lowering them, exclaimed, "O Allah (I do this), in Thy Belief, and in verification of Thy Book, and in Pursuance of Thy Prophet's Example—may Allah bless Him and preserve! O Allah, I extend my Hand to Thee, and great is my Desire to Thee! O accept Thou my Supplication, and diminish my Obstacles, and pity my Humiliation, and graciously grant me Thy Pardon!" After which, as we were still unable to reach the stone, we raised our hands to our ears, the palms facing the stone, as if touching it, recited the various religious formulae, the Takbir, the Tahlil, and the Hamdilah, blessed the Prophet, and kissed the finger-tips of the right hand. The Prophet used to weep when he touched the Black Stone, and said that it was the place for the pouring forth of tears. According to most authors, the second Caliph also used to kiss it. For this reason most Moslems, except the Shafe'i school, must touch the stone with both hands and apply their lips to it, or touch it with the fingers, which should be kissed, or rub the palms upon it, and afterwards draw them down the face. Under circumstances of difficulty, it is sufficient to stand before the stone, but the Prophet's Sunnat, or practice, was to touch it. Lucian mentions adoration of the sun by kissing the hand.

Then commenced the ceremony of *Tawáf*, or circumambulation, our route being the *Mataf*—the low oval of polished granite immediately surrounding the Ka'abah. I repeated, after my Mutawwif, or cicerone (guide), "In the Name of Allah, and Allah is omnipotent! I purpose to circuit seven circuits unto Almighty Allah, glorified and exalted!" This is technically called the Niyat (intention) of Tawaf. Then we began the prayer, "O Allah (I do this), in Thy Belief, and in Verification of Thy Book, and in Faithfulness of Thy Covenant, and in Perseverance of the Example of the Apostle Mohammed—may Allah bless Him and preserve!" till we reached the place Al-Multazem, between the corner of the Black Stone and the Ka'abah door. Here we ejaculated, "O Allah, Thou has Rights, so pardon my transgressing them." Opposite the door we repeated, "O Allah, verily the House is Thy House, and the Sanctuary Thy Sanctuary, and the Safeguard Thy Safeguard, and this is the Place of him who flies to Thee from (hell) Fire!" At the little building called Makam Ibrahim we said, "O Allah, verily this is the Place of Abraham, who took Refuge with and fled to Thee from the Fire!—O deny my Flesh and Blood, my Skin and Bones to the (eternal) Flames!" As we paced slowly round the north or Irak corner of the Ka'abah we exclaimed, "O Allah, verily I take Refuge with Thee from Polytheism, and Disobedience, and Hypocrisy, and evil Conversation, and evil Thoughts concerning Family, and Property, and Progeny!" When fronting the Mizab, or spout, we repeated the words, "O Allah, verily I beg of Thee Faith which shall not decline, and a Certainty which shall not perish, and the good Aid of Thy Prophet Mohammed—may Allah bless Him and preserve! O Allah, shadow me in Thy Shadow on that

Day when there is no Shade but Thy Shadow, and cause me to drink from the Cup of Thine Apostle Mohammed—may Allah bless Him and preserve!—that pleasant Draught after which is no Thirst to all Eternity, O Lord of Honour and Glory!" Turning the west corner, or the Rukn al-Shami, we exclaimed, "O Allah, make it an acceptable Pilgrimage, and a Forgiveness of Sins, and a laudable Endeavour, and a pleasant Action (in Thy sight), and a store which perisheth not, O Thou Glorious! O Thou Pardoner!" This was repeated thrice, till we arrived at the Yamani, or south corner, where, the crowd being less importunate, we touched the wall with the right hand, after the example of the Prophet, and kissed the finger-tips. Finally, between the south angle and that of the Black Stone, where our circuit would be completed, we said, "O Allah, verily I take Refuge with Thee from Infidelity, and I take Refuge with Thee from Want, and from the Tortures of the Tomb, and from the Troubles of Life and Death. And I fly to Thee from Ignominy in this World and the next, and I implore Thy Pardon for the Present and for the Future. O Lord, grant to me in this Life Prosperity, and in the next Life Prosperity, and save me from the Punishment of Fire."

Thus finished a Shaut, or single course round the house. Of these we performed the first three at the pace called Harwalah, very similar to the French *pas gymnastique*, or Tarammul, that is to say, "moving the shoulders as if walking in sand." The four latter are performed in Ta'ammul, slowly and leisurely; the reverse of the Sai, or running. These seven Ashwat, or courses, are called collectively one Usbu. The Moslem origin of this custom is too well known to require mention. After each Taufah or circuit, we, being unable to kiss or even to touch the Black Stone, fronted towards it, raised our hands to our ears, exclaimed, "In the Name of Allah, and Allah is omnipotent!" kissed our fingers, and resumed the ceremony of circumambulation, as before, with "Allah, in Thy Belief," &c.

At the conclusion of the Tawaf it was deemed advisable to attempt to kiss the stone. For a time I stood looking in despair at the swarming crowd of Badawi and other pilgrims that besieged it. But the boy Mohammed was equal to the occasion. During our circuit he had displayed a fiery zeal against heresy and schism, by foully abusing every Persian in his path; and the inopportune introduction of hard words into his prayers made the latter a strange patchwork; as "Ave Maria purissima,—arrah, don't ye be letting the pig at the pot,—sanctissima," and so forth. He might, for instance, be repeating "And I take Refuge with Thee from Ignominy in this World," when "O thou rejected one, son of the rejected!" would be the interpolation addressed to some long-bearded Khorasani,—"And in that to come"—"O hog and brother of a hoggess!" And so he continued till I wondered that none dared to turn and rend him. After vainly addressing the pilgrims, of whom nothing could be seen but a mosaic of occiputs and shoulder-blades, the boy Mohammed collected about half a dozen stalwart Meccans, with whose assistance, by sheer strength, we wedged our way into the thin and light-legged crowd. The Badawin turned round upon us like wild-cats, but they had no daggers. The season being autumn, they had not swelled themselves with milk for six months; and they had become such living mummies, that I could have managed single-handed half a dozen of them. After thus reaching the stone, despite popular indignation testified by impatient shouts, we monopolized the use of it for at least ten minutes. Whilst kissing it and rubbing hands and forehead upon it I narrowly observed it, and came away persuaded that it is

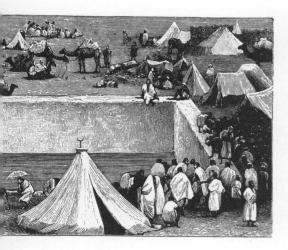

an aërolite. It is curious that almost all travellers agree upon one point, namely, that the stone is volcanic. Ali Bey calls it, "mineralogically" a "block of volcanic basalt, whose circumference is sprinkled with little crystals, pointed and straw-like, with rhombs of tile-red feldspath upon a dark background, like velvet or charcoal, except one of its protuberances, which is reddish." Burckhardt thought it was "a lava containing several small extraneous particles of a whitish and of a yellowish substance."

Having kissed the stone we fought our way through the crowd to the place called Al-Multazem. Here we pressed our stomachs, chests, and right cheeks to the Ka'abah, raising our arms high above our heads and exclaiming, "O Allah! O Lord of the Ancient House, free my Neck from Hell-fire, and preserve me from every ill Deed, and make me contented with that daily bread which Thou has given to me, and bless me in all Thou hast granted!" Then came the Istighfar, or begging of pardon: "I beg Pardon of Allah the most high, who, there is no other God but He, the Living, the Eternal, and until Him I repent myself!" After which we blessed the Prophet, and then asked for ourselves all that our souls most desired....

In the evening, accompanied by the boy Mohammed, and followed by Shaykh Nur, who carried a lantern and a praying-rug, I again repaired to the "Navel of the World"; this time aesthetically, to enjoy the delights of the hour after the "gaudy, babbling, and remorseful day." The moon, now approaching the full, tipped the brow of Abu Kubays, and lit up the spectacle with a more solemn light. In the midst stood the huge bier-like erection,—

> "Black as the wings
> Which some spirit of ill o'er a sepulchre flings,"—

except where the moonbeams streaked it like jets of silver falling upon the darkest marble. It formed the point of rest for the eye; the little, pagoda-like buildings and domes around it, with all their gilding and fretwork, vanished. One object, unique in appearance, stood in view—the temple of the one Allah, the God of Abraham, of Ishmael, and of their posterity. Sublime it was, and expressing by all the eloquence of fancy the grandeur of the One Idea which vitalised Al-Islam, and the strength and steadfastness of its votaries.

The oval pavement round the Ka'abah was crowded with men, women, and children, mostly divided into parties, which followed a Mutawwif; some walking staidly, and others running, whilst many stood in groups to prayer. What a scene of contrasts! Here stalked the Badawi woman, in her long black robe like a nun's serge, and poppy-coloured face-veil, pierced to show two fiercely flashing orbs. There an Indian woman, with her semi-Tartar features, nakedly hideous, and her thin legs, encased in wrinkled tights, hurried round the fane. Every now and then a corpse, borne upon its wooden shell, circuited the shrine by means of four bearers, whom other Moslems, as is the custom, occasionally relieved. A few fair-skinned Turks lounged about, looking cold and repulsive, as their wont is. In one place a fast Calcutta *Khitmugar* stood, with turban awry and arms akimbo, contemplating the view jauntily, as those "gentlemen's gentlemen" will do. In another, some poor wretch, with arms thrown on high, so that every part of his person might touch the Ka'abah, was clinging to the curtain and sobbing as though his heart would break....

Late in the evening I saw a negro in the state called Malbus—religious frenzy. To all appearance a Takruri, he was a fine and powerful man, as the numbers required to hold him testified. He threw his arms wildly about him, uttering shrill cries, which sounded like *lé lé lé lé*! and when held, he swayed his body, and waved his head from side to side, like a chained and furious elephant, straining out the deepest groans. The Africans appear unusually subject to this nervous state which, seen by the ignorant and the imaginative, would at once suggest "demoniacal possession." Either their organisation is more impressionable, or more probably, the hardships, privations, and fatigues endured whilst wearily traversing inhospitable wilds, and perilous seas, have exalted their imaginations to a pitch bordering upon frenzy. Often they are seen prostrate on the pavement, or clinging to the curtain, or rubbing their foreheads upon the stones, weeping bitterly, and pouring forth the wildest ejaculations.

That night I stayed in the Harim till two A.M., wishing to see if it would be empty. But the morrow was to witness the egress to Arafat; many, therefore, passed the hours of darkness in the Harim. Numerous parties of pilgrims sat upon their rugs, with lanterns in front of them, conversing, praying, and contemplating the Ka'abah. The cloisters were full of merchants, who resorted there to "talk shop," and to vend such holy goods as combs, tooth-sticks, and rosaries. Before ten P.M. I found no opportunity of praying the usual two prostrations over the grave of Ishmael. After waiting long and patiently, at last I was stepping into the vacant place, when another pilgrim rushed forward; the boy Mohammed, assisted by me, instantly seized him, and, despite his cries and struggles, taught him to wait. Till midnight we sat chatting with the different ciceroni who came up to offer their services. I could not help remarking their shabby and dirty clothes, and was informed that during pilgrimage, when splendour is liable to be spoiled, they wear out old dresses; and appear *endimanchés* for the Muharram fête, when most travellers have left the city. Presently my two companions, exhausted with fatigue, fell asleep; I went up to the Ka'abah, with the intention of "annexing" a bit of the torn old Kiswat or curtain, but too many eyes were looking on. At this season of the year the Kiswat is much tattered at the base, partly by pilgrims' fingers, and partly by the strain of the cord which confines it when the wind is blowing. It is considered a mere peccadillo to purloin a bit of the venerable stuff; but as the officers of the temple make money by selling it, they certainly would visit detection with an unmerciful application of the quarterstaff. The piece in my possession was given to me by the boy Mohammed before I left Meccah. Waistcoats cut out of the Kiswah still make the combatants invulnerable in battle, and are considered presents fit for princes. The Moslems generally try to secure a strip of this cloth as a mark for the Koran. . . .

At last sleep began to weigh heavily upon my eyelids. I awoke my companions, and in the dizziness of slumber they walked with me through the tall narrow street from the Bab al-Ziyadah to our home in the Shamiyah. The brilliant moonshine prevented our complaining, as other travellers have had reason to do, of the darkness and the difficulty of Meccah's streets. The town, too, appeared safe; there were no watchmen, and yet people slept everywhere upon cots placed opposite their open doors. Arrived at the house, we made some brief preparations for snatching a few hours' sleep upon the Mastabah, a place so stifling, that nothing but utter exhaustion could induce lethargy there.

RICHARD BURTON
Pilgrimage to Al-Madinah and Meccah, 1855

"GOD OF LOVE, WHAT A SIGHT!"

The hajj *journal of Hadji Khan and Wilfred Sparroy, published in the first decade of this century, is intriguing in that it records the pilgrimage through Muslim eyes—the first such account to appear in English. "We in Europe can hardly have an idea of the zeal and delight which animate the pilgrim to the holy places of Arabia," the authors observed—and for those unfamiliar with the works of Burckhardt and Burton, at any rate, this was undoubtedly true.*

Having encompassed the Ka'bah seven times, we stood hard by the tomb of Abraham and watched the pilgrims fighting to kiss the Black Stone. The wonder was that we had emerged from the tight scrimmage with a skin more or less whole. The perspiration oozed out of the pores in streams: laying hold of the fag end of my sacred habit I wiped my forehead. "You must not touch yourself," said Seyyid 'Ali; "it is a grievous sin." "Let your conscience rest in peace," I replied; "I will do penance by sacrificing a sheep."

The guide smiled. "There is no stain, however vile, but money shall blot it out. Would that I were a rich man!" "Thou fool," I cried, "how about the stain of superstition? Will money wipe it out, think you?" "Yá-Moulai," he whispered, "speak low. . . . Listen. It is easier to dig the heart out of a mountain with the sharp end of a needle than to remove ignorance from the mind of a mullá. However, the Course of Perseverance has yet to be trod. Come let us hop and be of good courage, for to-morrow we must go in procession to Arafat. We must begin again with Niyyat; that is, with a declaration of intention in front of the Black Stone, and after that we must proceed to Safá, and say our prayers there." "I ask pardon of Allah!" I shrilled. "Look, the people will be trodden under foot near the Black Stone!" The guide was silent, his eyes were turned to where the crowd was thickest. "Look," he said, "a man is down. They are trampling him to death. That has often happened. In 581 of the Hegira no less than eighty-four men were trodden to death inside the Ka'bah. In 972 of the Flight sixty-five men were suffocated through the pressure of the crowd in the Harem itself. . . . Praise Allah, the man is up again. . . . See, his friends are bearing him to a place of safety." . . .

God of love, what a sight! "He has achieved merit," said the guide, "except, it may be, in the eyes of the 'mother of his children.' She will cease to love him when she sees him. However, he may die, and thus she may be spared the shock of—did you—but what have I done to offend you?" My reply was curt. "I find your levity somewhat tedious," I said impatiently. The wag was irrepressible. He waxed argumentative suddenly, affirming that the snares of the heart are beauty of face and charm of voice. He bade me to look on his own manly countenance. I might believe it or not, but even he had been deceived more than once. What chance of keeping love, therefore, had the wretch whose face had been stamped as flat as the palm of his hand? "Listen, and I will hum you a song," he whispered, "but it must be low, since it concerns the heart, the theme of the poets, and not the soul, which is the concern of the priests. For my part I am on the side of the poets. Even in Mecca. The song is old. It was sung by Adam in the Garden of Eden after the Fall. I have found it true. . . .

"'Oh, heart of mine, how often canst thou trace
Thy aching wounds to one bright maiden's Face!
How often must, amid discordant din,
Another's Voice be toned to take you in!

"'Yet ah, my heart, among thy darling foes,
Was one that matched both Nightingale and Rose;
A Flow'r, she bloomed a day; a Bird, her flight
She winged . . . and turned the Day to endless Night.'"

"Alas, my poor heart, its disease is incurable, I fear. No matter. Safá awaits
our coming. We will go and 'declare our intention,' and then be off to the hill
of Purity. Let us skip and hop, for to-morrow we die. Yá-Allah! yá-Muhammad!" So, approaching as near as we could to the Black Stone, we closed our
eyes, giving it as our determination to run seven times between the platforms
of Safá and Marveh, and to recite the prescribed prayers at the appointed
places. It is considered an act of grace in the devout to proceed thence to the
Zem-Zem well, and, drawing a bucket of water by means of the windlass with
his own hands, to besprinkle therewith his head and back and stomach, after
which he should drink a handful of the water, repeating the following prayer:
"O Lord, I beseech Thee to make this draught for me a source of inexhaust-
ible knowledge, a vast livelihood, and a preventive of all pains and diseases."

Frequent allusion is made to this spring in Arabian and Persian literature.
Its water ranks second to that of Kúsar, a stream that runs in the Garden of
Paradise, keeping the grass ever green and the flowers ever blooming. The
prettiest ruby wine is compared by the poets to the water of Zem-Zem; for
they believe it to be the spring that "gushed out for the relief of Ishmael,"
when Hagar, his mother, wandered beside him in the wilderness. The story
goes that when she saw the bubbling water it was to call to her son, in the
Egyptian tongue, "Zem, zem!" ("Stay, stay!"). The taste of the water is difficult to describe, but it is certainly bitterish. My guide, to whom I had appealed in the matter, answered, saying, "Allah—may I be His sacrifice—has
made this water sacred, as you know. It is neither sweet nor bitter, neither
fresh nor salt, neither scented or stinking, but would appear in its taste to be
a mixture of all these qualities. In everything sacred there must be a mystery,
or how could the mullás live?" As to its attributes, they may be counted by
the hundred. There is no disease that it will not cure provided it be taken
with a "pure" conscience. It is as inspiring to a Muslim poet as that of Heli-
con to an unbeliever. It prolongs life and purifies the soul of him that drinks
it in unswerving obedience to God through the mediation of Muhammad.
The rich pilgrims carried gold or silver flasks in which they poured the precious water, keeping it as a preservative of health, or as a remedy in case of
sickness. An Indian Prince told me that he intended to keep his in order to
restore the eyesight of his brother, who had been unable to accompany him
on the pilgrimage. The Faithful bring their winding-sheets along with them
and wash them in the holy spring. Some Negroes from Zanzibar have the
honour to be the guardians of the well and the dispensers of its contents, and
they exact as much as twenty piastres from the poor pilgrims for the washing
of one of these winding-sheets, and ten times that amount from the rich.

Now, this practice of washing the grave-clothes stands in need of explanation. When a Muslim dies and is buried, he is received by a heavenly host,
who gives him notice of the coming of the two examiners, Nakir and Monker.
These are two angels as livid as death and as black as a putrid corpse, and
they proceed to question him concerning his faith, more especially as to the
unity of God and the apostleship of the Prophet. If he prove himself a true
Mussulman, he is suffered to rest in peace and is refreshed by the air of Para-

dise. But, if he be of a loose belief, he is gnawed and stung till the resurrection by ninety-nine dragons that have seven heads each, the earth pressing harder and harder on his body without, unfortunately, injuring the dragons. It is in order to escape from this torture that the pilgrims wash their winding-sheets, in the life-giving water of Zem-Zem, some of them taking the precaution to make assurance doubly certain by inscribing on the sheets, in coloured letters, the most sacred chapters of the Kurán. One of the pilgrims showed me a winding-sheet belonging to himself on which had been written in green ink every single chapter of the Book. The well is covered with a small square building crowned with a cupola and a crescent, and is paved inside with marble. There are four Chinese windlasses at the top of the shrine for drawing the water, and these are working all day long, the keepers having the greatest difficulty in restraining the ardour of the poor, tradition-ridden devouts, some of whom were wrought to such a pitch of blind fanaticism that it was as much as the Negroes could do to prevent them from flinging themselves into the well.

Since I had not the good fortune to win my way to the windlass, I took a jug of Zem-Zem water, making the attendant a present of ten piastres for it. Then, having performed the necessary ablutions, I went out by the old gate (on the thither side of the Place of Abraham) and ascended the stairs of Safá. We found the platform alive with pilgrims, and there, facing the Ka'bah, we had to pass in review all the blessings we had received from God during our lives, from the days of our birth upward. That done, we repeated seven times in an audible tone: "God is great. . . . I praise thee, O Lord! . . . There is no god but God. . . ." Three times: "There is no god but the one God; there is not anyone like unto Him. For His is the kingdom, and to Him do we lift up our praise. He is the giver of life and the giver of death. Death and life He bestoweth on all living creatures, but He dieth not, neither doth He sleep. He is almighty over everything. . . ."

The distance between the two hills is four hundred and thirty-eight yards. The course has to be traversed seven times. It begins at Safá and ends on the seventh lap at Marveh. Those who are too weak or too ill "to persevere" on foot must be carried on a horse, a camel, a mule, or a donkey, like the women, who, if sufficiently wealthy, are accompanied by three hired servants. The first, the forerunner, who clears the way, wears an expression of indescribable gravity. You can tell by his face that you have only to cast an eye behind him to behold a "Light of the Harem." The second, leading the beast by the bridle, looks religiously ahead, and the third brings up the rear, doing all in his power to protect his precious burden from the shrieking crowd. If a pilgrim at this stage of initiation allow his thoughts to dwell on the fair sex he must sacrifice a calf in the Valley of Mina. From the foot of Safá to the first minaret at the south-eastern end of the Harem the pilgrim must walk at his ease, and there he must say a prayer. It is this: "I begin in the name of God, and by God, and God is great. May peace be with Muhammad and with his household. O Lord, the compassionate and merciful, who art capable beyond my knowledge, O Thou who art most exalted and most generous, take this act of worship of mine, which is not worthy of Thee, and, enriching it with Thy abundance, make it more deserving of Thy acceptance. I offer up my 'perseverance' to Thee, O Lord, and in Thee my hope and strength are fixed. O Thou that acceptest the devotion of the pious, reject not my offering, O God." Thenceforward, until he reached the Baghleh Gate, some eighty yards away, the pilgrim had to suit his gait as far as in him lay to the rolling pace of a camel on the trot. He had now reached the starting point for hopping. Two big green flags were flying to give him warning. Up went the left leg of every mother's son and of many a father's daughter—for to every woman who rode there were twenty on foot—and a great deal of panting confusion and breathless excitement ensued. Hands were lifted to the sky, voices were raised in praise of God, asking for strength "to persevere," mules stampeded, horses lashed out with their heels, camels pierced their way through the surging mob as silently and as irresistibly as a ship breasts the sea, men and women being hurled aside like waves. The endurance displayed by the barefooted devout was marvellous. They were buoyed by the assurance that they were supported by the angels, Gabriel being the captain of the guard.

Now shoved forward by the pilgrims in the rear, now carried back by those who were returning from Marveh, I hopped about in a vicious circle, groaning and perspiring, like a man bereft of his senses. Should I never reach the blessed Gate of Ali! Who said the distance was not more than seventy-five yards? Let him hop over the course and he will multiply its figures by ten at every step. The folly of it all seemed to crash down on the crown of my bare head, shattering my belief in human sanity. For, carried away by the obligation of imitating the "persevering" antics of my fellow-pilgrims, I found myself now hopping on one leg like a melancholy heron, and now, on reaching Ali's Gate, pitching and rolling and labouring along like a spent camel under a goat. Yá-Allah! yá-Muhammad! I cut a sorry figure in my own estimation, no matter what merit I earned in the minds of my co-mates in affliction. So depressed was I that I had forgotten to say the prescribed prayer at the second minaret before reaching the Baghleh Gate: "O God, the possessor of praise and knowledge and mercy and magnanimity, pardon my trespasses, for, verily, there is no forgiver of sins but Thee alone." Many were maimed for life, not a few were killed, accident followed accident, but still the unheeding wave of pilgrims swept along over the fiery sand, shrieking and gesticulating, till my senses seemed to swoon. My guide, inured to the Arabian heat and to the unhallowed confusion of the course, performed his part with a studied dignity and a nimbleness of resource which added a touch of humour to an exhibition otherwise saddening. But these pilgrims themselves were tormented by no such self-accusing thoughts. If their feet were cut they had the consolation of believing that the streams of Paradise would wash them whole, for the cool water of Salsabíl and Tasním, if they succumbed to their devotional exertions, would it not be lifted to their parched lips by divine peris and everlasting life be theirs?

What might strike the spectator most of all would probably be the contrast presented by the dignity of the prayers and the occasional outbursts of religious extravagance on the part of the priest-ridden and ignorant among the pilgrims. The prayers might be read in any church in Christendom. The stormy outbursts from all reserve could only be witnessed nowadays in the East, where religion, that ship of salvation, though seaworthy enough in its undeniable if narrow sincerity, is in constant danger of being wrecked in the breakers of fanaticism. Muhammad reverenced science.... it was rated by him at its true value. The priests persist in disregarding its lessons from sheer self-interest. It is not the light of religion which they spread abroad. It is the fire of fanaticism which they fan—a fire which, by throwing out abundant heat but no light whatever, burns while diffusing darkness. "God does not change

the condition of people," said Muhammad, "until they change it for themselves." If these retrograde priests had kept themselves abreast of the times, as they were in duty bound to do as followers of a man of progressive genius, the crescent of Islám had been a wellnigh perfect round long ago. Enlightenment was not wanting on the part of a great number of laymen . . . but as to the greater number of the priests I met at Mecca, well, let us hope that, on ascending the platform of Marveh, they were conscious of falling short of the responsibilities of their office, and that they made amends by throwing into the prayer of repentance the burden of a contrite spirit: "O Lord, Thou that hast commanded to pardon; O Thou that forgivest with pardon; O Lord, pardon! pardon! pardon! pardon!" And if they could then weep out of the fulness of a heart ill at ease in its breast, and not perfunctorily as by law ordained, there might be some hope of their redemption. All joined in the concluding prayer, which runs: "O Lord, verily, I beseech Thee, in all circumstances, to endow me plentifully with tacit faith in Thee, and also to grant that I may be pure of intention in my resignation to Thy divine will."

HADJI KHAN AND WILFRED SPARROY
Pilgrimage to Mecca, 1905

THE MOSQUE
OF THE HARAM

"This book breaks no new ground," its author candidly informed readers when A. J. B. Wavell's Mecca *was issued in 1912. But noting that "a good many years have gone by since the last Englishman to intrude himself into those places told the story of his adventures," Wavell opined there was a place for his account alongside those of such giants as Burckhardt and Burton. Indeed there was, for Wavell visited Mecca during the height of the Turkish-Arab struggle for control of the Hijaz, a contest that ultimately claimed as many lives as the Boer War. Yet while the latter had been covered in exhaustive detail in the British press, the former had rated scarcely a mention. It was in part to redress this imbalance that Wavell wrote the following.*

We spent the next few days very pleasantly in exploring Mecca. There was much to see and do, and the crowded markets were a never-failing source of interest and amusement. Mecca is a very much bigger place than Medina: its normal population apart from pilgrims is said to be 70,000, though I should have put it myself at a much higher figure. It must be remembered however that the pilgrims there during the week of the Hag may number upwards of 500,000, and that for most of them house accommodation has to be provided, so that the number of buildings composing the city is greatly in excess of what would normally be required. The streets are, generally speaking, wide and clean, and the houses are nearly all three or four stories high—sometimes more. The principal markets are roofed, as in Damascus, and though they do not compare with those of that place in number or variety, there are nevertheless some very good shops. The merchants cater almost entirely for the pilgrims, most of whom like to take away with them some memento of their visit. There are no local industries whatever, and I quite failed to find anything that could be considered characteristic of the place itself. Goods are imported hither from all parts of the Orient—silks from Syria, carpets from Turkey and Persia, brass-work from India and Egypt—and all these things "go down" well enough with most of the pilgrims, but are the despair of the traveller who knows he could buy the same things better and cheaper in many much more accessible places than Mecca. Beside the resident merchants traders from all parts of Islam bring their wares to Mecca at this season, and are always certain of finding a ready market and doing a profitable business.

The government of Mecca is peculiar. It is really a semi-independent province of Turkey, under the rule of a "Shareef" who is invariably chosen from certain families descended from Ali and Fatima. This Shareef is considered to be an independent monarch: he lives in a palace, maintains a corps of guards, and has theoretically absolute powers within his own narrow dominions. He is treated with the same ceremony as the Sultan of Turkey or any other Eastern potentate. The lineage of the Shareefial families is supposed to be pure and irreproachable. In them one ought to see the Arab as he was in the days of the Prophet, before the Moslem conquests had introduced the foreign element which in these days is so apparent in most of them. The present Shareef is a man of about fifty, of medium height and good build. He has straight, regular features, a long, grey beard, and a rather dark complexion.

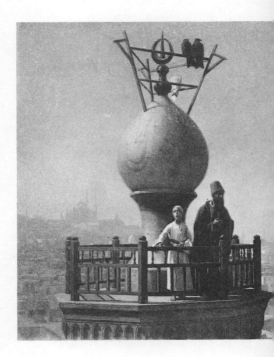

The Turks have a considerable garrison in Mecca, but I was unable to ascertain the exact number of troops. The big fort overlooking the town from the southwest should be capable of accommodating a couple of thousand at least. It looks a formidable work, almost impregnable to assault, but of course not adapted to withstand heavy artillery. Forts become obsolete nowadays almost as quickly as battleships. The public buildings of Mecca include a courthouse, post and telegraph and other Government offices. There are no monuments of interest except the somewhat doubtful relics of the Prophet which I shall describe presently. Beside the Haram there is only one other mosque in the town itself.

The climate of Mecca is not a pleasant one, though it is by no means unhealthy. It is very hot all the year round, and very dry. Rain falls only once or twice a year, but when it does fall it makes up for lost time. The town is so shut in by the surrounding hills that a breeze seldom reaches it, and the heat reflected from their rocky faces greatly increases the glare in the daytime and the stuffiness of the atmosphere at night. In the term of years during which the pilgrimage falls in the winter months it is customary for the Government and the wealthier citizens to remove themselves for the summer to Taif, a place about three days' journey to the south-east, which is much cooler, has a good water supply, and is comparatively fertile. The soil of Mecca is almost entirely barren; practically nothing, so far as I could see, grows anywhere in the neighbourhood. Its inhabitants depend exclusively on supplies from outside sources, and it was always a marvel to me where the food required for the enormous number of camels came from. There is, I suppose, a certain amount of grazing for them among the mountains.

The only true well in Mecca is the one in the Haram called "Zemzem," and the main water-supply of the town is derived from springs at Mount Arafat. The water is brought to Mecca by a conduit which runs through the town subterraneously, and is tapped at intervals by pits resembling wells. The water-drawers are a special class; they carry the water in skins and supply houses at a certain rate per month according to the quantity required. The water is of good quality when uncontaminated, and the supply is plentiful, except when the channel gets blocked up, as occasionally happens....

The people themselves in fact are the most interesting feature of the place.... while the pilgrimage to Mecca is compulsory for every Moslem that can manage it, the visit to Medina is purely for such as can afford the luxury, and not one quarter of those who come to the pilgrimage reach the latter

place. The concourse gathered together for the Friday prayer the week of the Hag is a sight worth the seeing.

Among all the pilgrims of different races daily pouring in, I was most struck by the Javanese. In appearance and manners they seem not unlike the Japanese. They have the same acquisitive and imitative temperament, are intensely curious regarding everything new to them, and quick to adopt any fresh idea that may seem to them an improvement on what has gone before. In this they stand in strong contrast to the Arabs, and in fact to most Eastern peoples, whose extreme conservatism is what really hinders their progress. But while the Japanese have seemingly agreed to take England as their model, the Javanese endeavor to turn themselves into Arabs. The first thing they do on arriving is to attire themselves in the local costume—which, by the way, does not suit them at all. I am told that there are so many people wearing Arab dress in Java that a stranger might fancy himself in the Hedjaz. Most of them seem very well-to-do, and they spend more money in Mecca than any other class of pilgrims. They often pay £100 for the use of a house at Mina for the three days of the pilgrimage. They are very keen Mohammedans, excellent linguists, and far better informed regarding current affairs than either Arabs or Turks. . . .

We several times visited the slave-market. Mecca is, I believe, one of the few places remaining where the trade is carried on thus openly. The slaves, who are kept in special show-rooms, sit, as a rule, in a row on a long bench placed on a raised platform. They are all women; male slaves and eunuchs may be bought by private treaty, but are not exposed in the market. One is ushered into each room by the proprietor, who expatiates the while on the "points" of his wares, and the phenomenally low price he is asking for them. One may, if so disposed, prod them in the ribs, examine their teeth or otherwise satisfy oneself that they are sound in wind and limb, which their owner is usually prepared to guarantee if desired. It is not usual, however, to warrant them free from vice—which would, moreover, merely have the effect of depreciating their value.

In making a purchase one may either close at the price stated or make an offer, which will be noted, and accepted if no better one is forthcoming within a certain stated time. This is a very usual method of selling goods of all kinds in Oriental countries.

The usual price for female slaves ranges from £20 to £100. In the case of Georgians and Circassians with special physical charms and educational accomplishments it is sometimes much more. I asked about these, but was told that none had been brought to Mecca this year owing to the high mortality among them from cholera the year before. All the merchants offered to get me one if I would give an order, and to guarantee that she should be up to specification; but I did not see my way to doing business on these terms. None of those we inspected would I have taken as a gift. . . .

We devoted a morning to the usual round of sightseeing, which here consists in viewing various relics of the Prophet and his family, all of them, I believe, of very doubtful authenticity. The first place of interest is a group of tombs some little distance outside the town on the left of the road going to Mina. Here are buried Khadijah, the Prophet's first wife, his uncle Abbas, Abu Talib, the father of the celebrated Ali, and one or two others less well known. In general these tombs resemble those in the Bakeia at Medina; but they are kept in slightly better repair. There is some difficulty about Abu Talib, as it is moderately certain that he died an unbeliever. He gets, however, the usual fatiha, in accordance with the tolerant spirit of the age. While visiting these tombs we were beset, as usual, by crowds of beggars, who caught hold of our clothes and absolutely declined to let us go forward till we distributed largesse. It is necessary to provide one's self for the purpose with a few handfuls of the small copper coinage known as "Nuhass," of which about a thousand go to the dollar.

On the way out we met a party of Indians, and agreed to "split" with them the cost of a Mutowif to take us round the tombs and other places we had to visit. One of these Indians was a large fat man dressed in European clothes, who told us he had been British Vice-Consul at some place on the Persian Gulf. He and Abdul Wahid conversed in English the whole time, the latter occasionally translating for my benefit. The Indian spoke English so well that apart from his appearance one would never have taken him for a foreigner; he seemed to know all about England and Zanzibar. He asked me if I did not find my total ignorance of English rather a nuisance; to which I replied that I had often thought of learning it, but had been deterred by the difficulty of the grammar.

This misplaced flippancy might have had serious consequences. I believe that before we managed to get rid of him he had formed in his own mind a conclusion concerning our party which was not very far from the truth. However, we heard no more of him.

The next place we visited, after leaving the tombs, was the house where the Prophet was born. We were shown a room in the basement which had in the middle of it a small iron structure hung with curtains. Here we knelt down in turn, and putting our heads through a hole in the hangings, were enabled to kiss a circular slab of marble which marks the exact spot where the event took place. The house itself is quite modern and most people are very skeptical as to the genuineness of its claims. For obvious reasons, stories relating to the early life of the Prophet and his followers have nothing like the same right to credence as those of his later years, which may for the most part be considered historical.

We next visited the house where Ali was born, and went through the same performance. I had always understood that he was born in the Kaaba, and our guide admitted that there was disagreement on the subject. Finally we were shown the house where Mohammed and his wife Khadijah lived together for so many years. This is really supposed to be genuine as regards its site, though the present building is new. The house being built in a sort of hole, one has to descend a flight of steps in order to reach the set of three rooms indicated as the historic apartments. In one of these we prayed a two-rukka prayer and read a passage from our guide-books containing some appropriate reflections. . . .

On the first of the month the "Ihram," a white linen band, was fastened round the black covering of the Kaaba. It remains till the day of the festival, when the "Kiswah," that is the covering itself, is changed. A new kiswah is brought every year with the Egyptian mahmal; it is sewn in Constantinople and is said to cost £3,600. The material is a mixture of silk and cotton, dull black in colour, and embroidered with the name of God worked in black silk about every square foot. The old one is cut up into pieces of varying sizes, which are sold for the benefit of the upkeep of the mosque and charitable purposes.

The Mosque of the Haram is unique in that it has no "Kibla" or prayer direction. The Kaaba itself being the object to which they turn, the worshippers at prayer form circles round it instead of the usual straight lines looking in the direction of Mecca.

It is possible to enter the Kaaba itself on certain occasions, and I had originally intended to do so. The rules regarding it however are stricter than formerly. Only men of mature age and of particularly blameless repute were allowed to go inside, so Abd-ur-Rahman told me. It was not proper to do so unless prepared to devote the rest of one's life to religious pursuits and renounce thenceforward the world, the flesh, and the devil. Since, however, he had himself been in, the old sinner may have intended this to be facetious. There is nothing whatever inside except a single wooden pillar. It so happened that it was never open when I was present: but Masaudi saw it open on two occasions, on one of which the Shareef and the governor of Mecca entered together and swept out the interior with brooms.

The mahmal arrived from Egypt at the beginning of the month, and with it a large contingent of Egyptian soldiers. It seemed strange to see the familiar khaki uniforms and medal ribbons in this place. I was pleased to see that their turn-out was very much smarter than that of the Turkish troops who came afterwards with the Syrian mahmal. It speaks well for British methods that they should have made such good soldiers out of so unwarlike a people as the modern Egyptians. Every one was impressed by the smartness of their uniforms and the precision of their drill.

It was now time to make preparations for the pilgrimage. We should be absent from Mecca for four whole days, and arrangements for transport and food supply had to be made. We agreed that it would not do in the circumstances to be too economical, and that our equipment had better be of a nature suitable to my supposed rank and wealth. We decided to hire three camels and three riding donkeys, and to take on one extra servant and another big tent in which to receive visitors. I gave Abdul Wahid *carte blanche* as regards the commissariat department, and he certainly "did us proud." We had lost the services of Ibrahim because he was performing a "pilgrimage by proxy." According to this idea a pilgrimage may be made on behalf of any dead person, and even in certain cases on behalf of one still living. Having arrived in Mecca and performed the towaf on his own account, the pilgrim must leave the city and change into the Ihram again somewhere outside. Thenceforward he performs all prayers and ceremonies in the name of the person he is representing. Many Sheia sects believe in the efficacy of this.

The institution of the "Hag" is as follows. On a certain fixed day in each year, the 8th of the month of Dhu'lhagga, all grown-up persons in a fit state of health must leave the city before nightfall and proceed to a village called Mina, about five miles to the north. They must pass the night here and go on the following morning to Mount Arafat, nine miles farther, where they must remain till the sun has set; then returning, they sleep at Nimrah, midway between Arafat and Mina. The third day they must get back to Mina in the morning, go through the ceremony of throwing stones at the three "devils," then go on to Mecca, perform the "towaf" and the "saa," and once more return to Mina for the night. The fourth day is the festival and is spent at Mina. At noon on the fifth they return to Mecca after once more throwing the stones. From the time of leaving Mecca up to the first return there, the Ihram is worn; but as soon as possible after leaving the Haram on that occasion, it is finally doffed and exchanged for the finest raiment the pilgrim can afford, which should if possible be brand new. Those who complete these ceremonies are thenceforward entitled to the appellation of Hagi before or after their names, and are distinguished in after life by special headgear which varies in different countries. In Egypt they wear green turbans, in Zanzibar the coloured straw hats and white turbans generally worn by the Mutowifs—and so on. I could never make out exactly at what point one becomes a "hagi." According to some, to arrive at Arafat on the appointed day is sufficient to confer the title; others think it dates from kissing the black stone at the end of the "towaf" ceremony on the third day. A man visiting Mecca outside the pilgrimage season, or one who was prevented by illness from performing these ceremonies on the proper days, would not be entitled to the distinction. The inhabitants of Mecca are not exempt from making the pilgrimage every year. They have to go forth with the rest, so that for two days the city is practically deserted.

It is not possible here to enter into the origin of all these rites, even were I capable of doing so efficiently. Suffice it to say that there is a *raison d'être* for everything. It is frequently contended that much of it is ridiculous; but precisely the same may be held by the sceptic to apply to any religious function. Like the "Lord's Supper" of the Christians, and the "Passover" of the Jews, these things are done in commemoration of past events and have a symbolic significance. Nothing is easier than to make fun of them all.

The question uppermost in the mind of every one just before the pilgrimage is whether there will be any sickness—that is to say, plague or cholera. In this particular pilgrimage the danger loomed larger than usual, owing to the terrible epidemic of the previous year. It seems that the disease appeared on that occasion about a month before the "Khuroog" (or "going out"), and steadily gained ground; but it was only after Arafat that it began to assume the gigantic proportions it finally attained. The pestilence then appeared in its most virulent form, and at Mina and during the succeeding week destroyed at the most generally accepted estimate a thousand a day. The recurrent peril of these devastating epidemics and the immense loss of life caused by them might be met to some extent by stringent regulations, preventing people setting out for Mecca without insufficient means, and by improving the sanitary conditions on the spot. The present quarantine system is useless.

This year, however, conditions were exceptionally favourable; the weather was unusually cool for the season, the number of pilgrims was not so large as usual, and there were fewer of the very poor, who, by camping in the open under most insanitary conditions, are always the focus of infection. So far as was known at the time of the Khuroog, no case of cholera or plague had occurred in Mecca, though two cases of the latter disease had been discovered in Jiddah. The bubonic plague, though equally deadly, is not nearly so much to be feared as cholera, owing to its comparatively slow rate of progress, and the fact that the multitude gathered together in Mecca, which is the source of danger, disperses almost immediately after the pilgrimage.

A. J. B. WAVELL
Mecca, 1912

REFERENCE

Chronology of Middle East History

*What follows is in no sense a complete chronology of Middle Eastern history.
The incidents and events listed below all relate, directly or indirectly, to the
history of Mecca and the buildings that comprise the Sacred Mosque.*

Entries in boldface refer specifically to Mecca.

A.D. 570   **Birth of Muhammad into the illustrious clan charged with guarding the Kaaba, Mecca's sacred shrine; Yemenite king invades Mecca, endows Kaaba with glass mosaics**

608   **Dilapidated Kaaba rebuilt with assistance of shipwrecked Byzantine carpenter; entrance raised to prevent flood waters from entering**

612   After receiving divine revelations on Mt. Hira, Muhammad begins his prophetic career

622   Hejira, or Migration, to Medina by Prophet and followers

624   Outnumbered Muslim forces defeat Meccan army at oasis of Badr

627   Meccan troops besiege Medina but are repulsed by Prophet's followers

628   Treaty of Hudaybiya grants Muhammad permission to make *hajj*, or pilgrimage to Mecca, in following year

630   **Capture of Mecca by Muslims**

632   Muhammad's death; his successor, Abu Bakr, chosen by acclamation

632–661   Orthodox caliphate

633   Khalid ibn Walid leads incursion into Iraq

634   Abu Bakr, the first Caliph, succumbs and is succeeded by Omar, who establishes primacy of Arabs over their tax-paying subjects; **both Caliphs buy and raze houses surrounding Kaaba**

635   Khalid conquers Syria, then occupies Iraq (637)

638   Capture of Jerusalem by Muslim soldiers

642   Final defeat of Persians; capitulation of Egypt to Muslims

644   Omar assassinated by Christian slave of governor of Basra

644–656   Uthman, notorious for his nepotism, orders official redaction of Koran and presents copies to major mosques

c. 650   **Abdullah ibn Zubair, contestant for caliphate, rebuilds Kaaba entirely after it catches fire**

656   Uthman slain while reading copy of standardized Koran; succeeded by Muhammad's cousin and son-in-law, Ali

661   Ali, last of the Companions of the Prophet, slain in great mosque of Kufa, Iraq

661–750   Omayyad caliphate; **Mecca and Medina known for sexual license**

c. 670   **Omayyad governor al-Hajjaj demolishes Zubair's Kaaba and reconstructs it along ancient lines**

673–78   Blockade of Constantinople by Muslim fleet ends in failure

c. 683   **Fire in Kaaba cracks Black Stone in three pieces**

711–15   Conquest of Spain by Muslim Moors

732   French army under Charles Martel defeats Abd ar-Rahman, governor of Spain, in battle of Tours, checking Muslim advance into Europe

745–46   **Kharijite revolt; Mecca seized by rebels**

750–c. 1100   Abbasid caliphate

775–85   **Reign of Caliph al-Mahdi, who imports pillars from Egypt to form colonnade around Kaaba**

786–809   **Haroun al-Rashid, most spectacular of Abbasid Caliphs and subject of many *Arabian Nights* tales, makes nine pilgrimages to Mecca from caliphal capital of Baghdad, contributes pulpit to Sacred Mosque**

930   **Fanatical Iraqi sect captures Mecca, slaughters 50,000 inhabitants, and carries off the Kaaba's legendary Black Stone**

951   **Black Stone returned to Mecca; its fragments set in silver boss**

968–1171   Fatimid dynasty in Egypt marked by extraordinary efflorescence of Muslim culture

995   Fatimids establish House of Science in Cairo

1096–1250   Period of the Crusades

1183–85   **Ibn Jubayr makes *hajj* to Mecca from Moorish Spain**

1201   **Ibn Arabi, renowned Sufi writer, makes *hajj*; attachment to learned woman in Mecca inspires love poetry**

1212   Moors expelled from Spain following battle of Las Navas de Tolosa

1258   Mongols sack Baghdad; Abbasid dynasty collapses

1258–1517   **Mameluke era; empty *mahmal*, a camel-borne pavilion, dispatched annually from Cairo to Mecca as symbol of subservience**

1260   Victory of Mamelukes at Ain Jalut checks Mongol advance and preserves Egypt as last refuge of Muslim culture

1291   Saladin consolidates power over Egypt, Nubia, Yemen, and the Hijaz

1326	Rise of Ottoman Turks in northwest Anatolia	**1916**	**Beginning of Arab revolt in Hijaz; Ottoman troops in Mecca surrender; Mecca's Sharif, Hussein, proclaimed king of the Arabs**
1453	Siege and capture of Constantinople by Muhammad the Conqueror, real founder of Ottoman empire, ending 1,000 years of Byzantine rule	**1900–08**	**Construction of the Hijaz Railroad, linking Baghdad and Mecca**
1503	**Ludovico Bartema visits Mecca from native Italy via Syria, traveling with caravan of 40,000 pilgrims**	1917	Arabs under T. E. Lawrence take Aqaba; harassment of Hijaz Railroad guards, interrupting Turkish communications in Middle East; Balfour Declaration proposes creation of state of Israel in Palestine; Bolshevik government reveals that Britain has made conflicting promises to Hussein, Jews, and French
1517	**Ottoman army defeats Mamelukes, occupies Egypt and Hijaz; Sharif of Mecca surrenders voluntarily**	1918	Feisal enters Damascus at head of Arab army; 400 years of Ottoman rule end; Hussein, refusing to accept Balfour Declaration, is deposed; **Mecca loses status as capital of Arabia;** Turks surrender Hijaz Railroad head at Medina
1529	First siege of Vienna by Turks		
1571	Battle of Lepanto, greatest naval battle since Actium; Ottoman fleet destroyed or captured by European armada	1919	Abd al-Aziz ibn Saud secures first victory in Hijaz
1585	Beginning of decline of Ottoman empire	1923	Transjordan organized as autonomous state under Hussein's son Abdullah
1683	Turkish troops under Grand Vizier Kara Mustafa besiege Vienna but are repelled; deepest Ottoman incursion into Europe	**1924**	**Ibn Saud and his troops take Mecca; Hussein abdicates in favor of eldest son, Ali, who flees Hijaz some months later**
c. 1790	**Muhammad Abdul Wahhab preaches return to purity of early Islam; Wahhab and followers capture Islam's holy places, hang their red *kiswa*, or drapery, over the Kaaba (1806)**	1926	Ibn Saud proclaimed king of Hijaz
		1932	Kingdom of Hijaz renamed Saudi Arabia
1798	Napoleon Bonaparte's Egyptian expedition	1933	United States receives first concession to develop Arabia's oil resources
1801–30	Greek war of independence	1938	Oil discovered at Dhahran
1810–18	**Muhammad Ali leads campaign to clear Hijaz of Wahhabis; enters Mecca**	1956	Nasser nationalizes Suez Canal, provoking international crisis leading to Israeli invasion of Egypt
1811	Muhammad Ali, Macedonian Muslim, sent by sultan to organize Egyptian resistance to French; massacres Mamelukes in Cairo citadel	1958	Feisal succeeds deposed brother, ibn Saud
1814	**John Lewis Burckhardt, a Swiss-German adventurer, enters Mecca disguised as Sheikh Ibrahim ibn Abdullah**	**c. 1965**	**Station of Ibrahim reduced in size and enclosed; entire superstructure of Zemzem, Mecca's sacred well, removed**
1817	Burckhardt perishes of fever in Cairo; his *Travels in Arabia* published posthumously in London (1829)	1966	Six-Day War
c. 1830	**Sir Richard Burton, eminent Victorian explorer and writer, reaches Mecca disguised as a Persian holy man, Mirza Abdullah; recounts his adventures in *Pilgrimage to Al-Madinah and Meccah* (1855)**	**c. 1968**	**Construction of Saudi Mosque, which encircles older Ottoman structure**
		c. 1970	Hajj Research Centre established at Jiddah
		1973	October War against Israel; first oil boycott embargo
1869	Opening of Suez Canal; Ottoman empire once more on main trade routes to Far East	**1979**	**Muslim fanatics seize Sacred Mosque and Kaaba by force of arms; Saudi officials put down insurrection with much loss of life but only minor damage to structure; rebels summarily executed**
1874	Collapse of Ottoman empire enters final phase		
1882	Great Britain begins "temporary" occupation of Ottoman Egypt—which lasts into 1950s		
1885	Sudanese Muslim known as the Mahdi captures Khartoum, massacres garrison		

Guide to the Pilgrimage

Where does the Pilgrimage begin? For most Muslims, it begins years before the actual journey, during childhood, when they are taught to answer the traditional call to prayer with the words *"Allahu Akbar, Allahu Akbar*—God is most great."* All Muslims know that call is a holy command, a divine summons. But to understand the true meaning of the call to prayer, the believer has to make the pilgrimage at least once in his life.

The *hajj,* or pilgrimage, is the fifth pillar of Islam—the other four being *Shadada,* faith; *Du'a* and *Salat,* prayer; *sadaqa* and *zakat,* alms; and *Ramadan,* fasting. Since the Prophet Muhammad's Pilgrimage of Farewell in A.D. 632, uncounted millions of pilgrims have made the *hajj,* a journey that, until recently, was often an odyssey involving incredible adventures. Pilgrim caravans from Egypt took almost two months crossing the Sinai Desert, risking attack by Bedouins. The other great caravan assembled in Damascus, and those travelers journeyed for as long as thirty days to Mecca. These caravans were like vast, moving cities under the command of soldiers and civil servants, with upwards of 6,000 pilgrims traveling in one group. So many people under the presence of a benign command considerably reduced the risks that might be encountered on the journey, but pilgrims from other lands had no such advantages. Unable to join a caravan, they made the pilgrimage in the face of appalling odds, and overcame hazards that would have daunted the less devout, crossing every kind of terrain from desert to jungle, and often taking years to arrive. (One man, single when he left his far-off homeland, arrived in Mecca with a wife and several children. Another man, a child when he started, was in his seventies when he arrived.)

The poor made the journey in stages, stopping to work every so often to pay their way. Some were enslaved and many died—not unhappily, in some cases, since death while on the pilgrimage is said to guarantee entry into Paradise. Even in the early years of this century the suffering of pilgrims did not end when they reached Mecca: banditry, profiteering, and excessive taxation were common; medical and sanitary conditions outrageously inadequate.

No such fortitude is required of today's pilgrims. The Saudi Arabian government has invested millions of ryals in modern transport, shelter, and hygiene to make the pilgrimage physically comfortable, and as a result more than two million of the 800 million Muslims across the world are able to obey the call each year. Less than forty years ago, the pilgrimage drew a mere 108,000 souls; today it is a miracle of faith and organization, the world's most astonishing peacetime logistical exercise. Pilgrims arrive in Jiddah in an unceasing stream, coming in huge jet planes and ocean-going liners. (In the peak days of the pilgrim season, almost one million passengers land at Jiddah airport from all over the world.) Many are illiterate peasants who have devoted their life savings to the journey; a few are men of wealth. On the road to Mecca, however, they are joined in a common bond of obedience to the world of the Prophet, who said: "Know that every Muslim is every Muslim's brother. Nothing belonging to his brother is lawful to man, unless it be given freely and with good grace...."

When they arrive in Saudi Arabia, pilgrims complete their preparations for their visit to the Holy City. There is a rigid ritual for each stage of the pilgrimage, and these rites are to be followed without deviation. It is possible for a pilgrim to complete the pilgrimage within the proscribed five days, which begin on the eighth day of Dhul-Hijja, the month set aside for the pilgrimage, but almost every pilgrim allows himself at least two weeks for this great event, which climaxes on the ninth day of Dhul-Hijja with the mass migration to Arafat.

The crowds that throng the specially built Pilgrim City on the outskirts of Jiddah form a vivid splash of white, for most are already wearing the traditional pilgrim garb, two pieces of seamless white cloth known as *ihram*. The word *ihram* refers both to the garment and the special duties it imposes on the pilgrim. The white cloth is a symbol of the pilgrim's search for spiritual purity, a mark of chastity. Once he has donned it, the pilgrim enters the state of *ihram*, in which he may not adorn himself with jewelry or other decorations, involve himself in argument or dispute, commit violence, or have sexual relations. Before putting on *ihram* the pilgrim must wash himself, cut his nails, trim his moustache, shave the hair from his armpits and pubic area, perfume himself, and don sandals. (Women can perform the *hajj* in respectable clothing of any color.) When he puts on *ihram*, the pilgrim performs two prostrations and recites two prayers. He then declares

which form of pilgrimage he intends to make.

The *'Umrah*, or Lesser Pilgrimage, can be performed at any time of the year, and most Muslim visitors to Jiddah also travel to Mecca for this act of devotion, which involves circumambulating the Kaaba and running to and fro between the hills of Shafa and Marwa. There are, in addition, three forms of the Main Pilgrimage: *Qiran*, conjunction; *Tamattu*, gratification; and *Ifrad*, singularity. In the first, the Main Pilgrimage and the *'Umrah* are performed together, the rites of the *'Umrah* being included in the act of the Main Pilgrimage. In the second, the pilgrim performs the *'Umrah* before he performs the Main Pilgrimage. And in the third, the pilgrim performs only the Main Pilgrimage.

For most pilgrims, Jiddah is but the first stage of the journey, a resting place from which to set out for Mecca. The millions in Jiddah merge into the corridor of pious sound that forms the road from Jiddah to Mecca, making each of the forty-five miles an affirmation of man's relationship with God. And always, through the days and nights of this most solemn event, the faithful offer up the *Talbiyah*, as they have done from time immemorial:

Here am I, O God, at Thy
   Command, Here I am!
Thou art without associates,
Thine are praise and grace and
   dominion
Thou art without associates
Here I am!

The end of this corridor of dedication is Mecca, where the pilgrim finally

sets eyes on the Sacred Mosque (**1**, diagram on p. 166). It is preferable to enter the Sacred House through the *Bab-as-Salam*, the Gate of Peace (**2**). During the first minutes in the mosque, many are overwhelmed at the sight of such a mass of people. The crowd is so orderly and restrained that newcomers pause in wonderment before raising their hands as their fathers and forefathers did in time gone by, crying out: "O God, You are peace, and peace comes from You. So, greet us, O our Lord, with peace."

This is a time of intense emotional fervor for most pilgrims, a time of stillness they they feel a blessed peace falling upon them. Here the *hajji* first performs the *tawaf*, seven counterclockwise circuits around the Kaaba (**3**), starting each time with the Black Stone. The pilgrim makes the first three rounds of the Kaaba at a fast pace, preferably with short steps; the remainder, at walking pace. (Women are not required to comply with this tradition, and the lame and sick are carried.)

After performing the *tawaf*, the pilgrim moves to the Station of Ibrahim (**4**), where he prostrates himself twice before moving on to the sacred well, Zemzem (**5**). From Zemzem the pilgrim crosses to the hills of Shafa and Marwa (**6**), the symbols of patience and perseverance, where he walks briskly between two designated signs.

Every year on the seventh day of Dhul-Hijja, a ceremony is held to wash the Kaaba. The king of Saudi Arabia, the servent of the mosque, performs this symbolic act of humility under the watchful eyes of thousands of pilgrims and various heads of state of Islamic

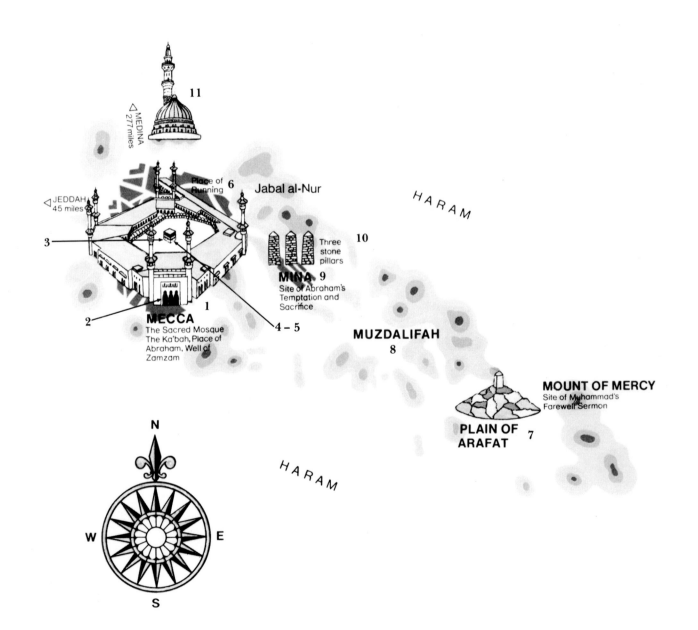

JEDDAH
45 miles

MEDINA
277 miles

11

Place of
Running **6**

Jabal al-Nur

HARAM

3

Three
stone
pillars

10

1

2

MINA 9
Site of Abraham's
Temptation and
Sacrifice

4 – 5

MECCA
The Sacred Mosque
The Ka'bah, Place of
Abraham, Well of
Zamzam

MUZDALIFAH
8

MOUNT OF MERCY
Site of Muhammad's
Farewell Sermon

PLAIN OF
ARAFAT **7**

HARAM

N

W   E

S

countries and chiefs of Islamic missions. After the king has performed this washing ceremony he holds a reception for the dignitaries.

At this point the pilgrimage is still only half completed; there remains the most impressive demonstration of faith to be witnessed on the face of the earth—the day when more than two million people gather on the Plains of Arafat (**7**). All at Arafat are in a state of dedication. When the sun crosses the meridian and travels beyond its zenith, the imam preaches a sermon, followed by midday and afternoon prayers. The words of God echo in the minds of the faithful—"All of you are the descendants of Adam, and Adam was of clay"—just as they did during the Prophet Muhammad's last sermon, more than 1,400 years ago. It was after his farewell sermon that Muhammad rode to a pile of rocks where, legend has it, Adam sought God's mercy after he first sinned. Watched by the vast crowds which had gathered to hear him, he remained seated on his camel, his head bowed in thought. Near sunset, the Prophet sagged forward, oblivious of the crowd. He was receiving one of his last divine messages. Then, at sunset, he raised himself in the saddle and rode on to Muzdalifa (**8**), where fires had been lit to guide him. Today, the pilgrim reenacts all these solemn events, kneeling and prostrating himself at Muzdalifa and performing shortened versions of both the sunset and evening prayers.

This spot, another open plain, lies roughly halfway between Arafat and Mina (**9**) and is an important place in Islamic history for it marks the place where the Prophet rested and prayed after his ride from Arafat. Here, until midnight, the pilgrim prays and rests and gathers the stones he will hurl at three whitewashed pillars in Mina. These pillars are thought to represent devils, commemorating the time when Satan cajoled Abraham and sought to make him defy God's command to sacrifice Ishmael. Thus, throwing the stones symbolizes the pilgrim's rejection of evil. The exodus to Mina begins after midnight when the massive crowd of pilgrims makes its way to the ancient town where the three pillars stand (**10**). They are encircled by immense pedestrian ways on two levels, on which the pilgrim can stand to perform the ceremony. Each person should have either forty-nine or seventy stones no smaller than a chick pea, but no bigger than a hazelnut.

On the morning of the tenth day the pilgrim casts seven of his stones at the Great Devil, *Jamrat al-Aqabah*, calling out with each throw: "*Allahu Akbar*—God is most great." On the next day the pilgrim stones all three devils, throwing seven stones at each pillar as custom demands. The final stoning takes place on the third and last day, again at all three pillars. The stoning is symbolic of man's casting out evil from himself, seeking God's help for any time in the future when the devil may try to tempt him. Confident that God is greater than all other powers, the pilgrim will be able to resist the temptation. The stones cannot be thrown haphazardly—any pilgrim who misses the target has to repeat the stoning.

The feast of *Idd al-Adha*, which follows, is the most joyous occasion in Islam. This feast is celebrated by Muslims all over the world, not just by those on the pilgrimage. The *hajjis*, once out of the *ihram*, don their brightest, most colorful clothes, and joyful crowds throng Mina, bartering and joking. When the negotiations with shepherds and herdsmen are completed, the pilgrim leads a newly bought animal away for the sacrificial rites. Finally, when it is time to leave, the pilgrim goes to the Sacred Mosque for the last time and performs the farewell *tawaf*.

The pilgrimage, as devotion and ritual, is at an end, but there remains one more journey which all pilgrims long to make—a visit to the Prophet's Mosque, 277 miles to the north in Medina, the second holiest city in Islam and a place revered by all Muslims (**11**). The pilgrim enters the Prophet's Mosque and prays, performing two prostrations as a greeting. Now he faces the Prophet's grave and says: "Peace be upon You, O Messenger of God, peace be upon You, O Prophet of God, peace be upon You, O most exalted of God's creatures, peace be upon You, Messenger of God who is Lord of the world." After that he retreats a small way to the right and faces the grave of Abu Bakr, Muhammad's closest friend, to greet him in prayer. Then he moves again, a little farther, to stand before the grave of the Commander of the Faithful, Omar ibn al-Khattab. Once these dedications are completed, the pilgrim bows in prayer for his family, his friends, his Muslim brothers, and himself.

For many pilgrims, a visit to Medina and the Mosque of the Prophet is the only way to end the pilgrimage, bearing in mind Muhammad's words: "One prayer in my Mosque is better than a thousand in another, excepting the Holy Mosque of Mecca."

Selected Bibliography

Burckhardt, John Lewis. *Travels in Arabia*. London, 1829.
Burton, Richard. *Pilgrimmage to Al-Madinah and Meccah*. London, 1855.
Creswell, K.A.C. *A Short Account of Early Muslim Architecture*. Pelican, London, 1938.
Dickson, H.R.P. *The Arab of the Desert*. Allen and Unwin, London, 1939.
Hitti, Philip K. *History of the Arabs*. Macmillan, London, 1937.
Nicholson, R.A. *A Literary History of the Arabs*. T. Fisher Unwin, London, 1907.
Ralli, Augustus. *Christians at Mecca*. Heinemann, London, 1909.
Sanger, Richard H. *The Arabian Peninsula*. Cornell University Press, New York, 1954.
The Shorter Encyclopaedia of Islam. Brill, Leiden, 1953.
Watts, Montgomery. *Muhammad at Mecca*. Oxford, 1956.
———. *Muhammad at Medina*. Oxford, 1956.

Acknowledgments and Picture Credits

The Editors would like to thank Clyde Leamaster of the Ministry of Education in Riyadh, Saudi Arabia, for the assistance he provided in preparing this volume for publication. In addition, the Editors would like to thank the following individuals and organizations:

Charlie Holland, Spencer Collection, New York Public Library. Elizabeth Ashley, Joseph T. Rankin, and Mary Daugherty, Metropolitan Museum of Art, New York.

All the modern photographs of Mecca in Mecca are the work of Mohamed Amin. The title or description of all the other pictures appears after the page number (boldface), followed by its location.

HALF TITLE Symbol by Jay J. Smith **9** Tile showing the Kaaba, Turkey, 18th century. Victoria and Albert Museum (Michael Holford) **12** Miniature of the Ascension of Muhammad from a Persian manuscript, 16th century. Collection Trunifer, Lucerne (Giraudon)

CHAPTER 1 **19** Map by Wilhelmina Reyinga **20** Miniature of the Kaaba from a pilgrim scroll, 15th century. British Library, Ms. Add 27566

CHAPTER 2 **25** Miniature of Arab soldiers, *Seances de Hariri*, 1237. Bibliothèque Nationale, Paris, Ms. Arabe 5847 fol 19 **26** Miniature of Arabs in a tent, *Seances de Hariri*, 1237. Bibliothèque Nationale, Paris, Ms. Arab 5847 fol 139v **27** Stele, Saudi Arabia, c. 2nd century. Louvre **30** Prayer rug, 16th century. Metropolitan Museum of Art **31** Mosque lamp, Egypt, 1250 Metropolitan Museum of Art **33** Miniature of Seventh Heaven. Bibliothèque Nationale, Paris

CHAPTER 3 **36–40,44** All miniatures from Darir, *Siyar-i Nabi*, 16th century. Spencer Collection, New York Public Library **50** Miniature of Mongol troops from Rashid-al-din' *Jami al-Tawarikh*, 1314. Edinburgh University Library, Ms. 20 fol 122 **51** Miniature of Muhammad on horseback accepting surrender of a tribe, 1306. British Library Mss. Or. 4 fol 3 **54** Miniature of Muhammad restoring the black stone from Rashid-al-Din, *Jami al-Tawarikh*, 1314. Edinburgh University Library, Ms. 20 fol 55 **55** Miniature of Ali at the Kaaba from Darir, *Siyar-i Nabi*, 16th century. Spencer Collection, New York Public Library **56** Miniature from Darir, *Siyar-i-Nabi*, 16th century. Spencer Collection, New York Public Library **57** Miniature of Muhammad's ascension to Heaven on al-Buraq. British Library

CHAPTER 5 **76–77** Gate in the western façade of the Great Mosque, Cordoba (Oronoz)**–78–79** Interior of Hagia Sophia, Istanbul (Ara Guler) **86–87** Both: Richard Burton, *Pilgrimage to . . . Mecca*, London, 1855. New York Public Library

CHAPTER 6 **95** Brass astrolabe, Yemenite, 13th century. Metropolitan Museum of Art, Bequest of Edward C. Moore, 1891 **97** George Cruikshank, *Flight from Egypt*, London, 1815. **103** J. L. Burckhardt, *Travels in Arabia*, 1829. New York Public Library **104** Caricature of Sir Richard Burton by Carlo Bellegrini, 1885. The Granger Collection **105** Richard Burton, *Pilgrimage to . . . Mecca*, London, 1855 New York Public Library

CHAPTER 7 **108–109** All: The Granger Collection **110** John Sergeant, *Arab Woman*. Metropolitan Museum of Art, 111 Jean Léon Gerôme, *Prayer in the Mosque*. Metropolitan Museum of Art, Bequest of Catharine Wolfe, 1887.**–112–115** All: T. E. Lawrence, *The Seven Pillars of Wisdom*, London, 1926. Rare Book Division, New York Public Library

MECCA IN LITERATURE **136–160** 19th-century engravings of Mecca and surroundings. New York Public Library

Index

Christmas Tree!

For David and Stephen

—W.M.

For Judy Stevens and her Christmas spirit

—F.M.

Christmas Tree!
Copyright © 2005 by Wendell and Florence Minor
Manufactured in China.

Library of Congress Cataloging-in-Publication Data
Minor, Wendell.
  Christmas tree! / Wendell and Florence Minor.— 1st ed.
    p. cm.
  Summary: Christmas trees come in all shapes and sizes and can be found
in almost any setting, but there is only one "best" Christmas tree.
  Includes bibliographical references.
  ISBN 0-06-056054-7 — ISBN 0-06-056055-5 (lib. bdg.)
  [1. Christmas trees—Fiction. 2. Christmas—Fiction. 3. Stories in rhyme.]
I. Minor, Florence Friedmann. II. Title.
PZ8.3.M6467Ch 2005   2004022755
[E]—dc22   CIP
                                          AC

Typography by Wendell Minor and Al Cetta
1 2 3 4 5 6 7 8 9 10 ❖ First Edition

Christmas Tree!

WENDELL AND FLORENCE MINOR

KATHERINE TEGEN BOOKS

An Imprint of HarperCollinsPublishers

Christmas
is
here!
Imagine
that you are
a Christmas tree.
What kind of tree do
you think you could be?

A tree so
high it would
touch the sky?

Or a tree
so small it would
fit in the wall?

A tree
that would sing
when Christmas
bells ring?

Or a tree
so bright
it would light
up the night?

A tree that was made for a city parade?

Or a tree
that's at home where
the buffalo roam?

A tree
that could
float on
top of a
boat?

$\mathbf{A}$ tree
just
for dogs,

Or one
that's for
cats,

Or one just for horses— how about that?

A tree where
there's snow,

r
there's
lots
of sunshine ...

No!
The
best tree
of all is the
one that is mine!

MERRY CHRISTMAS

A Few Little-Known Facts about Christmas Trees

The
oldest
known record
of a Christmas
tree is from 1551, in
Strasbourg,
Germany.
Decorations on early
Christmas trees consisted
of mostly candy,
fruit, and nuts.
Candles were used to light up
Christmas trees beginning in 1708.
The first known Christmas tree in America
was in Bethlehem, Pennsylvania, in 1746.
The first record of a Christmas tree in a large
American city is from Philadelphia, in 1825.
Christmas trees were first displayed in Boston in 1832,
Texas in 1846,
and San Francisco in 1862.
In the 1890s, tradition held that Santa Claus brought
children a Christmas tree along with their toys on Christmas Eve.
Only one in five American homes had a Christmas tree in 1900.
By 1930, Christmas trees could be seen all across America.
Electric lights first appeared on a Christmas tree in America in 1901, and they have been
keeping Christmas bright ever since.

SOURCE

Snyder, Phillip V., *The Christmas Tree Book: The History of the Christmas Tree and Antique Christmas Tree Ornaments* (New York: The Viking Press, 1976).